Organize Your Books in 6 Easy Steps

A Workbook for the Sole Proprietor Service-Oriented Business

Donna M. Murphy

IRIE PUBLISHING
Fort Collins, Colorado

Organize Your Books in 6 Easy Steps
A Workbook for the Sole Proprietor Service-Oriented Business
Copyright © 1998 by Donna M. Murphy

This publication is designed to provide accurate and authoritative information regarding the subject matter at hand. It is sold with the understanding that the publisher and author are not engaged in rendering legal or accounting services. If legal advice is required, the services of a competent attorney should be sought.

Published by IRIE Publishing: 301 Boardwalk Drive
P.O. Box 273123
Fort Collins, CO 80527-3123
iriepub@verinet.com (e-mail)

IRIE Publishing and the author make no representations or warranties with respect to the accuracy or completeness of the contents of this book and shall in no event be liable for any damages, including but not limited to direct, special, incidental, consequential, or other damages.

Editorial Assistants: Sue Maksen, Patrick A. Murphy
Illustrations: Jennifer Clarke

All rights reserved. No part of this book, including interior design, cover design, and illustrations, may be reproduced or transmitted in any form, by any means (electronic, photocopying, recording, or otherwise) without the prior written permission from IRIE Publishing.

Library of Congress Catalog Card Number: 98-93133
ISBN: 0-9664848-0-0

Publisher's Cataloging-in-Publication
(Provided by Quality Books, Inc.)

Murphy, Donna Marie
    Organize your books in 6 easy steps: a work book for the sole proprietor service-oriented business/by Donna M. Murphy ; [editorial assistants Sue Maksen, Patrick A. Murphy ; illustrations by Jennifer Clarke].
    p. cm.
    Includes bibliographical references and index.
    Preassigned LCCN: 98-93133
    ISBN: 0-9664848-0-0

    1. Bookkeeping.   I. Title. II. Title: Organize your books in six easy steps

HF5635.M87 1998   657'.2
                               QBI98-903

Printed in the United States of America

DEDICATIONS

This book is dedicated to my sole support, my confidant,
my soul mate, my partner.

ACKNOWLEDGMENTS

I first and foremost would like to thank my husband, Patrick and my children, Brendan, Alana and Fallon for being the ultimate foundation for me and my dreams.

I would also like to thank Sue Maksen, a friend and colleague who has helped me through this entire process. Without Sue, I would not have known where to begin. Additionally, thanks to Jennifer Clarke, a wonderful illustrator who helped make this workbook and my life more fun.

To my friends Karen D. and Toni who have been my emotional support throughout this endeavor, as well as other endeavors, I thank you both.

To all of my friends and family who participated in the creation of this workbook, thank you for your encouragement and inputs.

TABLE OF CONTENTS

List of Figures vii
Preface viii

INTRODUCTION 1
Prerequisites for using this workbook • Revisiting the sole proprietor • What is a service-oriented business? • Iconology • Checklist 1: Preliminary business preparations • Checklist 2: Recordkeeping necessities • The bottom line

STEP ONE: Understand the Purpose of Your Books 11
Two primary reasons to keep records • More supporting evidence for keeping records • When to enlist help • Single entry vs. Double entry

STEP TWO: Identify Your Recordkeeping Needs 17
Accounting period (calendar vs. fiscal) • Accounting methods (cash vs. accrual) • Determine which records to create • Exercise 1: Working with income • Exercise 2: Working with expenses • Exercise 3: Keeping track of your petty cash • Exercise 4: Tracking your fixed assets for depreciation • Exercise 5: Keeping track of accounts receivable • Exercise 6: Keeping track of accounts payable • Exercise 7: Tracking transportation expenses • Exercise 8: Tracking travel expenses • Exercise 9: Tracking meals and entertainment expenses • Exercise 10: Determining your net worth

STEP THREE: Compile Client and Vendor Records 43

STEP FOUR: Create a Service List 49

STEP FIVE: Generate Reports 53
Income summary • Expense summary • Balance sheet • Profit and loss statement • Sample recordkeeping schedule

STEP SIX: Keep the IRS Happy 61
Schedule C/C-EZ, Profit or Loss from Business or Profession • Schedule SE, Self-Employment Tax • Form 1040-ES, Estimated Tax • Form 4562, Depreciation and Amortization • Form 8829, Expenses for Business Use of Your Home • Sole Proprietor tax schedule

Let's Recheck Our Steps 66

Recordkeeping Troubleshooting 68

Appendix A: Worksheets 73

Appendix B: References and Resources 91
Books • Periodicals and Publications • Accounting Software • Websites • Other Sources of Assistance

Appendix C: Suggested IRS Publications 99

Appendix D: IRS Tax Forms 103

Appendix E: Jargon 133

Index 139

LIST OF FIGURES

1. Sample Income Record 25
2. Sample Expense Record 27
3. Sample Petty Cash Record 29
4. Sample Fixed Assets Record 31
5. Sample Accounts Receivable Record 32
6. Sample Accounts Payable Record 33
7. Sample Transportation Record 35
8. Sample Travel Record 37
9. Sample Meals & Entertainment Record 39
10. Sample Balance Sheet 41
11. Sample Client Information 46
12. Sample Vendor Information 47
13. Sample Service List 52
14. Sample Income Summary 56
15. Sample Expense Summary 57
16. Sample Profit and Loss Statement 59
17. Sample Tax Calendar for the Sole Proprietor 65

PREFACE

I opened the doors to my home-based, researching and consulting business in March 1997, after spending nearly a decade in the computer software industry. While deciding which records I needed to keep for my business, I came to the unfortunate conclusion there were not many books specifically geared toward my business needs. Yes, plenty of books are available on recordkeeping and small business accounting. But few have actually scaled their information down to the level that meets the basic needs of the sole proprietor service-oriented business.

More small business owners are assuming control of their own business affairs — and this includes the onerous task of recordkeeping. Advances in accounting software have made it enticing for businesses to take financial matters into their own hands. This is not to say there is no longer a need for bookkeepers or accountants. These professionals still play an integral part in the recordkeeping process and should continue to be used as resources.

This workbook is intended to be a guideline. Use it as a starting point to help get your business records in order. Then, each time you're required to generate monthly, quarterly or yearly reports, you're prepared. And with your organized books in hand, tax season won't appear so daunting. Keep in mind that this is not Accounting 101! The goal of this book is to help you "organize" your business records.

"Good order is the foundation of all things."
— Edmund Burke

INTRODUCTION

The following is a list of prerequisites for using this workbook.
1. You are a sole proprietor.
2. You are primarily a service-oriented business.
3. You have **no** employees.
4. You file or plan to file Schedule C as part of Federal Tax Form 1040.
5. You've done a little dabbling with recordkeeping on your own.
6. You haven't organized your recordkeeping paperwork yet.
7. You're just not sure you even want to organize your records.

> ### STOP!
> If you do not meet the above prerequisites, this workbook is not for you. Please pass it on to a friend. Otherwise, keep reading.

Recordkeeping for a business can be tedious and frustrating; however, it doesn't have to be if you start with the right tools. I spent many hours and dollars looking for the right system for my researching and consulting business. I found very little out there that *really* caters to my specific type of business — the service-oriented sole proprietor. That is why I decided to create this hands-on workbook.

This workbook presents a six step system that will help your business stay on top of the books. It is not meant to be the cure-all for your business recordkeeping; its just a start to get you organized and keep you abreast of your business' financial situation. Even with this workbook in hand, it's always a good idea to get the advice of a bookkeeper or accountant. They will ensure that you are headed in the right direction and that you are not running afoul of any laws.

Don't be afraid to take control of your own books. Recordkeeping is fairly straightforward for the sole proprietor. And, for the sole proprietor running a service-oriented business, its the easiest recordkeeping of all the business structures!

Revisiting the Sole Proprietor

If you have read this far, you are probably a sole proprietor (or know someone who is) and know the requirements of being a sole proprietor. But for the sake of clarity let's revisit the definition of a sole proprietor and the advantages and disadvantages that go along with this type of business structure.

A sole proprietorship is defined as a business that is run solely by one person. In some cases, a married couple can be considered a sole proprietor. The IRS does not allow any other two-party situations to be sole proprietors. As a sole proprietor, you and your business are one in the same. According to the IRS, approximately 80% of businesses are started as sole proprietors. The primary reasons are: simplicity, ease of starting, and low cost of startup. Other advantages that make being a sole proprietor so attractive include: little, to no government regulations on the structure of your business, you do not have to answer to anyone else, and recordkeeping required for the sole proprietor is minimal.

With all of the advantages to being a sole proprietor come some disadvantages. A major disadvantage to being a sole proprietor is that you personally are liable for any financial liabilities leveled against your business. It is also quite difficult to borrow money from lenders as a sole proprietor and often requires that you put personal assets (e.g., your house, your car, etc.) up as collateral. Additionally, sole proprietors do not usually get the benefits (i.e., medical insurance, dental, child care, etc.).

Introduction

What is a service-oriented business?

A service-oriented business is one that provides primarily services (for a fee) to it's clients as opposed to producing and selling a product. According to the IRS there are over 18 million small businesses that report returns and of those, approximately 13 million were sole proprietors running service-oriented businesses.

The service-oriented business has characteristics that are advantageous to the small and home-based business owner. These same characteristics fit hand in hand with being a sole proprietor. The following are examples of what makes a service business so attractive:

1. **No inventory**, since you are selling a service.
2. **Minimal to no start-up costs** required for equipment or supplies.
3. **Low profile** and minimal disruption to neighbors and other businesses.
4. Can be kept as a **small-scale operation** — only one person need run it.
5. **Easier to compete** based on time and skill requirements.
6. **Growth potential** due to high demand of service businesses.

Some Common Service-Oriented Businesses

Accountant	Interior Designer
Calendar Service	Medical Billing Service
Cleaning Service	Office Support Service
Consulting (of any kind)	Pet-Sitting Service
Copywriter	Physical Therapy
Day Care	Professional Organizer
Desktop Publishing	Plant Service
Editorial Services	Referral Service
Errand Service	Technical Writer

Event Planner	Tax Preparation Service
Financial Planner	Temporary Help Agency
House Inspector	Word Processing Service

Service businesses are often categorized into either personal services or corporate services. Both categories were represented in the list above. Personal services are performed with the intention of serving individuals to enhance the quality of their life. These types of services may include: financial planner, plant service, interior designer, cleaning service, and event planner. The corporate service business concentrates primarily on businesses or corporations. This area of service is becoming more common due to the downsizing of corporations. As a result, these firms are turning to outsourced alternatives. Services for the corporate category might include: word processing service, technical writer, desktop publishing, editorial services or an errand service.

You can still benefit from this workbook if you primarily sell products, but have a part of your business providing services. Recordkeeping is a requirement for all business types. The only difference between a business which combines service with product sales and a service business will be the amount and type of records you will need.

"I do not believe you can do today's job with yesterday's methods and be in business tomorrow."

— Nelson Jackson

This workbook is designed to assist you in doing your books by hand. I recommend that you do your books this way first (i.e., by hand), so that you understand how your money is transacted through various accounts. It will also give you a better appreciation for automation! It's a great learning process even if you only do it once.

This workbook will walk through the following six steps of organizing your books. Samples throughout this workbook show how to fill in the worksheets that are provided in Appendix A. Once you have completed these six steps, you should have a well organized set of business records.

STEP 1: Understand the purpose of your books

STEP 2: Identify your recordkeeping needs

STEP 3: Compile client and vendor records

STEP 4: Create a service list

STEP 5: Generate reports

STEP 6: Keep the IRS happy

After you've worked through your books by hand (using the above six steps), you can then load that accounting software you purchased. Many accounting software packages (*see* Appendix B – References and Resources) on the market today are helpful tools. Testing a few of these packages will provide additional insight into the recordkeeping process. Some companies provide free trial offers of their accounting software. Take advantage of these offers so you can test the systems completely. Be careful when you decide to buy your software—many of these accounting software packages have extra bells and whistles you probably don't need. Don't spend extra money on these features.

Iconology

I have included helpful tips, things to remember and words of encouragement throughout this workbook. I hope these icon incentives keep you interested, motivated and forging ahead!

Tips: Little bits of information that may be helpful in your venture toward organizing your business records. I provide insights into what I do for my business as well.

Things to Remember: Things to stop you in your tracks and make sure that you either put it on your to do list, or make a mental note to do further research on the that particular topic.

Words of Encouragement: It's hard to take on such an endeavor without additional support. Look for words of encouragement throughout the workbook to keep you forging onward and boost your confidence.

Introduction

Checklist 1: Preliminary Business Preparations

- Make sure you separate your personal and business finances. It will make it easier to keep track of everything. You can still use this workbook even if you haven't separated your accounts yet.

- At a minimum, establish a business checking account.

  I also keep a business savings account to put away money for quarterly taxes and other regular repayment items.

- You may want to apply for a business credit card.

- Determine if you will be doing your books by hand, by computer or both. This workbook requires that you to do your books the first time by hand.

- If you plan on using accounting software to do your books, contact a local CPA or bookkeeper (or both) to get their recommendation.

- Are you legal? It's never too late to apply for a business license from city hall! Also check with your state for any additional licensing requirements.

- If there are CPAs or bookkeepers in your area that offer free consultations, take them up on their offer—and don't forget to bring all of your recordkeeping questions.

- Make sure you have a business or tax identification number. Sole proprietors, without employees, can use their Social Security number.

- Check with local city and county governments regarding any special business regulations, taxes and zoning restrictions that may apply to your business.

Checklist 2: Recordkeeping Necessities

- Get an accordion file that is divided by month. This is ideal for keeping receipts separated.

- Gather up some pens, pencils, a calculator and a stapler. Make sure the stapler is full!

- Find a LARGE area to spread out receipts, worksheets, bills, checks and the like. This area should NOT be accessible to small children or pets. "The dog ate it" will not work with the IRS!

- Get a three-ring binder (preferably with file pockets) that has dividers. Label each divider by month, quarter or year. Then store your information accordingly after you've completed the six steps.

- Have a minimum of four hours set aside to work from Step 1 through Step 6. You can, however, break the steps down over the course of a week if you don't have that kind of time in one day. And most of us don't!

"The beginning is the most important part of any work."

— Plato

Introduction

The Bottom Line

The benefit of organizing your books is twofold. First, it will save you time over the long haul. The initial time required to organize and gather information for recordkeeping is often miscalculated and underestimated. This puts recordkeeping on the bottom of the priority pile, resulting in a cram course in financial organization. But after your initial investment, the time required to maintain your books on a periodic basis is minimal compared to those year-end bookkeeping marathons! You may decide to turn this task over to your accountant or bookkeeper, but remember, it can be a costly expense.

This brings me to the second benefit of organizing your books—it will save you money! The amount of time your accountant or bookkeeper spends organizing your paperwork can be eliminated by your diligence. Take the four hours that I've suggested in this workbook to get your business records organized. Multiply those four hours by the hourly charge your accountant or bookkeeper receives. Now multiply that number by four (for each quarter of the calendar year) and then by the number of years you expect to be in business. It becomes clear just how much money you will save with this initial six step investment.

Remember, by organizing your business records up front (even though you may eventually send them off to an accountant, bookkeeper or tax preparer):

You *will* save TIME!

and

You *will* save $$$!

"Out of intense complexities, intense simplicities emerge."
— Winston Churchill

If you are feeling overwhelmed about the process of organizing your business records, this workbook will help. Organizing and maintaining records is one of the most difficult and challenging tasks that a small business owner faces. But, the importance of accurate and organized financial records cannot be stressed enough. Take this workbook and the time suggested to setup and organize your records. The initial time and energy will most definitely payoff in the end. And just think, the next time you need to create periodic reports or gather information for your taxes, it's all there for you. That's the beauty of this system!

"It is best to do things systematically, since we are only human, and disorder is our worst enemy."

— Richmond Lattimore

STEP 1
Understand the Purpose of Your Books

STEP 1 ACTIVITIES:

- Identify two primary reasons to keep records
- List more supporting evidence for keeping records
- A brief discussion on enlisting help
- Define single entry accounting
- Define double entry accounting

Step 1: Understand the Purpose of Your Books

Two primary reasons to keep records are:
    1. To track the trend of your business; and
    2. To provide a readily available source for tax preparation.

Why would you want to track the trend of your business? Well, by glancing through your records, you can quickly spot which areas were productive and cost-effective for your business and which areas were not. This will allow you to make better decisions about your business needs in future years giving your business a better chance for success.

How do your business records provide the information you need for tax purposes? As you go through the next steps of this workbook, you will be compiling pertinent information that will be used to fill out your tax forms.

More supporting evidence for keeping records
Now that we've considered the two primary reasons to keep records, here are some additional reasons that reinforce the importance of keeping records.

    1. Your records facilitate the handling of your receipts. This will help differentiate between business and personal items as well as taxable and nontaxable items.

    2. Your records provide a means to track deductible expenses so that you don't have to go on an archaeological dig through all the receipts and scraps of paper when it's time for tax preparation.

    3. Your records provide written evidence of items reported on your tax return. If you are asked by the IRS to have your return examined, you will be required to explain the item(s) in question. Keeping a complete and organized set of records will make this process less intimidating.

When to enlist help

Will you need help with your recordkeeping? This is entirely up to you. Even if you enlist the help of an accountant or a bookkeeper, I suggest you still be fully involved in the creation and maintenance of your books. By maintaining your own records, you will be on top of your business transactions. You will probably do your own books if you are just starting a small business and cannot afford to pay someone else to handle your recordkeeping. The exercise of preparing your books yourself is well worth the time and energy.

Not all service-oriented businesses are alike! Many have different recordkeeping requirements. Use this workbook as a guideline for what will work best for your business.

Single Entry vs. Double Entry

Most recordkeeping and accounting books now make the distinction between single entry and double entry accounting systems. The double entry system has been considered the traditional form of accounting, but as more home-based and small businesses perform their own accounting tasks, it has become acceptable for these types of businesses to use the single entry system. Depending on the complexity of your business you may be required to know both systems. Although both are accurate recordkeeping systems double entry has a built-in double check feature. Each will be briefly discussed here. For this workbook, however, the single entry system will be the default.

Single Entry: The single entry system is the method of accounting that uses only income and expenses. The beauty of this system is that you do not need a degree in accounting to use it! This system requires maintaining income and expense records, which are two of several records we will be creating in this workbook.

Step 1: Understand the Purpose of Your Books

Incidentally, the IRS also recommends the single entry system for beginning small businesses, especially sole proprietors (see IRS Publication #538 – Accounting Periods and Methods).

Double Entry: The double entry system is the method of accounting that accounts for every transaction twice. This means that every transaction has two sides and both sides always have to be balanced. The main records used by double entry accounting are called the *General Journal* and the *General Ledger*.

> *General Journal.* The general journal is used to record all transactions for a business in chronological order. A transaction is recorded as both a debit and a credit, balancing each other out.
>
> *General Ledger.* Entries made into the general journal now need to get posted into their individual accounts. This is done with the general ledger. Each transaction on the journal is recorded in detail to the ledger, grouped under its appropriate account, be it income or expense.

Familiarize yourself with both single entry and double entry systems! If you start by using the single entry system, you might have to switch to double entry as your business grows.

Lucky you – I didn't impose any exercises or strenuous activities on you in Step 1! Those impositions will start with the next step. This first step, however, is still an important step towards organizing your books. You need to understand why you are creating these records in the first place as well as how to begin setting them up. The concept of single entry accounting vs. double entry accounting is important to understand because it will dictate the amount of recordkeeping you will need to do.

As you start into Step 2, keep in mind that an investment of hard work and diligence yields a better existence. You are about to embark on an intense and activity-filled journey. Step 2 will require the most amount of time, so be patience and stick with it!

"If all difficulties were known at the outset of a long journey, most of us would never start out at all."

— Dan Rather

STEP 2
Identify Your Recordkeeping Needs

STEP 2 ACTIVITIES:

- Determine accounting periods (calendar vs. fiscal)
- Determine accounting methods (cash vs. accrual)
- Create income record
- Create expense record
- Create petty cash record
- Create fixed assets record
- Create accounts receiveable record
- Create accounts payable record
- Create transportation record
- Create travel record
- Create meals & entertainment record
- Generate a preliminary balance sheet
- Determine your net worth

Step 2: Identify Your Recordkeeping Needs

Identify your recordkeeping needs before you begin the task of organizing your books. Determine your needs by answering the following questions and going through some exercises. Once you have completed the questions and exercises, you are well on your way!

Question 1: Which tax calendar will you use?

Your tax calendar is the annual accounting period that will be used to keep and record your income and expenses. There are two accounting periods known as the calendar year and the fiscal year. You select your tax calendar when you file your first income tax return.

The calendar tax year is the twelve consecutive months beginning January 1 and ending December 31. You are required to use the calendar tax year if any of the following is applicable:

1. You do not currently keep adequate records for your business;
2. You have not specified an annual accounting period; or
3. Your present tax calendar does not qualify as a fiscal year.

The fiscal tax year is twelve consecutive months ending on the last day of any month except December. You should use the fiscal year if either of the following apply:

1. You currently keep adequate business records; or
2. You report your income and expenses using the same tax calendar.

The IRS says that for sole proprietors, your business tax year must be the same as your individual tax year.

Once you have adopted your accounting period, you must continue to use it. If you need to change your tax calendar for any reason, permission from the IRS is required and a fee (ranging from $100 to $250) will be charged. A sample form (Form 1128 – *Application to Adopt, Change or Retain a Tax Year*) is shown in Appendix D – IRS Tax Forms.

Question 2: What type of accounting method will you use?

An accounting method is a standard of rules used to determine how you will report income and expenses. The accounting method is decided when you file your first tax return associated with your business. There are four different accounting methods: cash, accrual, special and combination or hybrid.

Most sole proprietor service-oriented businesses use the cash method. This is primarily because of its simplicity and because taxes are paid only on the cash received. With the cash accounting method, income is recorded when cash is received, and a deduction is recorded when the expense is paid. This means that if you use the cash accounting method, your income and expenses will not match the actual dates of transactions (i.e., when it occurred).

>   *Income example:* You completed a project for a client and submitted an invoice to them on December 5, 1997. You then received a check from that client on January 5, 1998. That income should be recorded for 1998 taxes.

>   *Expense example:* You received the monthly telephone bill on December 15, 1997. The due date of the bill is January 15, 1998. You write a check to pay the bill on January 12, 1998 — the expense is considered a 1998 deduction.

If your business uses inventory, you must use the accrual method of accounting. The accrual method provides for a better match between revenue and expenses with actual dates of transactions. With the accrual accounting method, income is recorded when earned (not when received) and expenses are deducted as they are incurred (not as they are paid).

Step 2: Identify Your Recordkeeping Needs 21

Income example: You conducted a seminar for a company on December 10, 1997 and billed them on December 15, 1997. You didn't receive payment until January 20, 1998. The income is still recorded as 1997 income because that is when you actually earned it.

Expense example: You purchased business cards, letterhead and other office supplies from an office supply catalog in October 1997. You are not billed until December 1997 and pay in January 1998. You deduct this as an expense for 1997 since that is when it was incurred.

In this workbook we will use the cash accounting method. We're going for simple!

There may be certain aspects of your business income or expenses that are considered special methods of accounting. For example, you may have special requirements for depreciation, deductions for bad debts, installment sales or farming requirements. If this is the case, then you will need to follow the rules of the special method of accounting. IRS Publications #225 – *Farmer's Tax Guide*, #535 – *Business Expenses*, #537 – *Installment Sales* and #946 – *How to Depreciate Property* should be referenced for additional information on deciding to use the special method.

The combination or hybrid method is any combination of cash, accrual or special method. There are restrictions that apply to this method. Make sure to refer to IRS Publications #334 – *Tax Guide for Small Business* and #538 – *Accounting Periods and Methods* for a list of these restrictions.

If you need to change your accounting method, the IRS requires you to fill out Form 3115 – *Application for Change in Accounting Method*. This form has to be filed during the tax year for which the change is requested.

Question 3: What records do you need to create and maintain?

What types of items do you want to track for your business? Make a list of the items for which you will need to keep financial records. Think about the most logical things you need to track. Here are a few questions to get you started:

1. How much money do you make?
2. What are your expenditures?
3. Who owes you money?
4. To whom do you owe money?
5. What do you do with small cash expenditures?
6. How do you track the cost of your computer?
7. Do you provide pickup or delivery services?
8. Does your business require you to travel?
9. Do you meet clients at eating establishments?

> *Record* **n.** — Anything that is written down and preserved; anything that serves as evidence to an event.

"Discipline is the bridge between goals and accomplishments."
— Jim Rohn

Step 2: Identify Your Recordkeeping Needs

Now that you've given it some thought, you should have an idea of the items you want to track with your "records." For ease of discussion, let's put names to these records:

Question	Designated Record
How much money do you make?	Income
What are your expenditures?	Expense
Who owes you money?	Accounts Receivable
Who do you owe money?	Accounts Payable
What do you do with small cash expenditures?	Petty Cash
How do you track the cost of your computer?	Fixed Assets
Do you provide pickup or delivery services?	Transportation
Do you travel to conventions or seminars?	Travel
Do you meet clients at eating establishments?	Meals/Entertainm't

All the previously listed records together help determine what your business is worth. Information from these records will be incorporated onto a balance sheet. From the balance sheet, you will then be able to determine your net worth.

The idea here is to start basic and then add details as you get more comfortable doing your books. Keeping it basic in the beginning keeps you from feeling overwhelmed and less likely to give up. You'll be creating a record for each of the categories identified above, so you can see how things will come together.

Feel free to make multiple copies of the worksheets provided in Appendix A. They make good practice sheets.

EXERCISE 1: Working with Income.

Your business income is figured on the basis of your tax calendar and your accounting period. The IRS identifies items which can be considered as business income as well as items specifically not considered business income.

Valid Business Income	*Invalid Business Income*
1. Property or Services	1. Loans
2. Real Estate Rents	2. Appreciation
3. Personal Property Rents	3. Leasehold Improvements
4. Interest and Dividends	4. Exchange of Property
5. Canceled Debts	5. Consignments
6. Excluded Debts	6. Construction Allowances
7. Other Income	7. Retail Space

See IRS Publication #334 - *Tax Guide for Small Business* for additional types of income and brief explanations of both the valid and invalid business incomes shown above.

Even if you are moonlighting, you can have business income.

For the type of business used in this workbook (i.e., sole proprietor service-oriented), the income source(s) will be limited to services and fees. You may, however, want to divide your services into more detail so you can track from which specific service categories your income is derived. The information contained on your income record will be used later to prepare a profit and loss statement in Step 5. Figure 1 shows a sample income record generated for Dakota Consulting at the end of the third quarter.

INCOME RECORD

Company: Dakota Consulting   Date: 09/30/98

Reference	Date	Transaction	Income (Service/Fees)	Total
dc-0004	09/01/98	Donald P. Shriver, seminar preparation	$222.00	
		Donald P. Shriver, fees	$9.75	$231.75
dc-0001	09/05/98	Justin Case, techincal writing	$225.00	$225.00
dc-0002	09/12/98	CSA Incorporated, seminar	$1,290	
		CSA Incorporated, fees	$10.95	$1300.95
dc-0006	09/15/98	Brendan Architect, technical writing	$76.00	$76.00
dc-0002	09/22/98	CSA Incorporated, followup	$34.78	
		CSA Incorporated, fees	$0.78	$34.78
dc-0013	09/26/98	Margaret Queen, consultation	$320.00	
		Margaret Queen, fees	$2.10	$322.10
dc-0025	09/30/98	Altura Associates, techincal writing	$193.00	$193.00

Figure 1- Sample Income Record

EXERCISE 2: Working with Expenses.

The operating costs required to run your business are considered business expenses and can be deducted on your tax return. According to the IRS, in order for an expense to be deductible it must be *both* ordinary and necessary.

Ordinary expense: An expense that is common, unquestionable and accepted as related to your business.

Necessary expense: An expense that is used for operation of your business that is deemed appropriate and helpful.

Examples of what the IRS considers both valid and invalid business expenses are shown below. Again, refer to IRS Publication #334 – *Tax Guide for Small Business* for explanations of each.

Valid Business Expenses	*Invalid Business Expenses*
1. Bad Debt	1. Bribes
2. Car & Truck	2. Start-up Costs
3. Depreciation	3. Charitable Contributions
4. Insurance	4. Lobbying expenses
5. Interest	5. Penalties and fines
6. Legal & Professional Fees	6. Political contributions
7. Other Expenses	7. Repairs

An expense record is used to keep track of all your business expenditures. You should spend a good amount of time deciding the appropriate categories to use for your business. Figure 2 uses the following categories: advertising; postage; office supplies; utilities; and miscellaneous.

Step 2: Identify Your Recordkeeping Needs

EXPENSE RECORD

Company: Dakota Consulting   Date: 09/30/98

Reference	Date	Transaction	Advertis.	Postage & Handling	Office Supplies	Utilities	Misc.
Chk # 530	09/01/98	Donald P. Shriver		$9.75			
Chk # 531	09/03/98	Petty Cash					$50.00
Chk #532	09/11/98	Mtn. Plains Telecomm				$33.60	
Chk #533	09/11/98	CSA Incorporated		$10.95			
AMEX	09/15/98	Mountain Online					$12.95
Chk #534	09/21/98	Nixon Paper			$32.14		
AMEX	09/30/98	Jones Promotions	$101.25				

Figure 2 - Sample Expense Record

An expense record is helpful for tracking particular categories of expenditures and for responding to that tracking. For example, say that Dakota Consulting's budget for advertising is $75.00 per quarter. You can see from the data presented in Figure 2 above that the budget has been exceeded for the third quarter. However, Dakota Consulting can now make an adjustment to the advertising budget for the fourth quarter to accommodate the third quarter overage.

Use Schedule C, Part II (see Appendix D – IRS Tax Forms) as a template for your expense categories. Part II of this form will dictate the types of expenses to be itemized for tax purposes.

EXERCISE 3: *Keeping Track of Your Petty Cash.*

Petty cash can wreak all kinds of havoc on your business if you don't have a thorough petty cash system. A major problem that can arise due to improper usage of petty cash is the misrepresentation of your business' true financial status. The purpose of petty cash is to have cash-on-hand readily available for those business purchases too small to warrant writing a business check. The flow diagram below walks you through setting up your petty cash system.

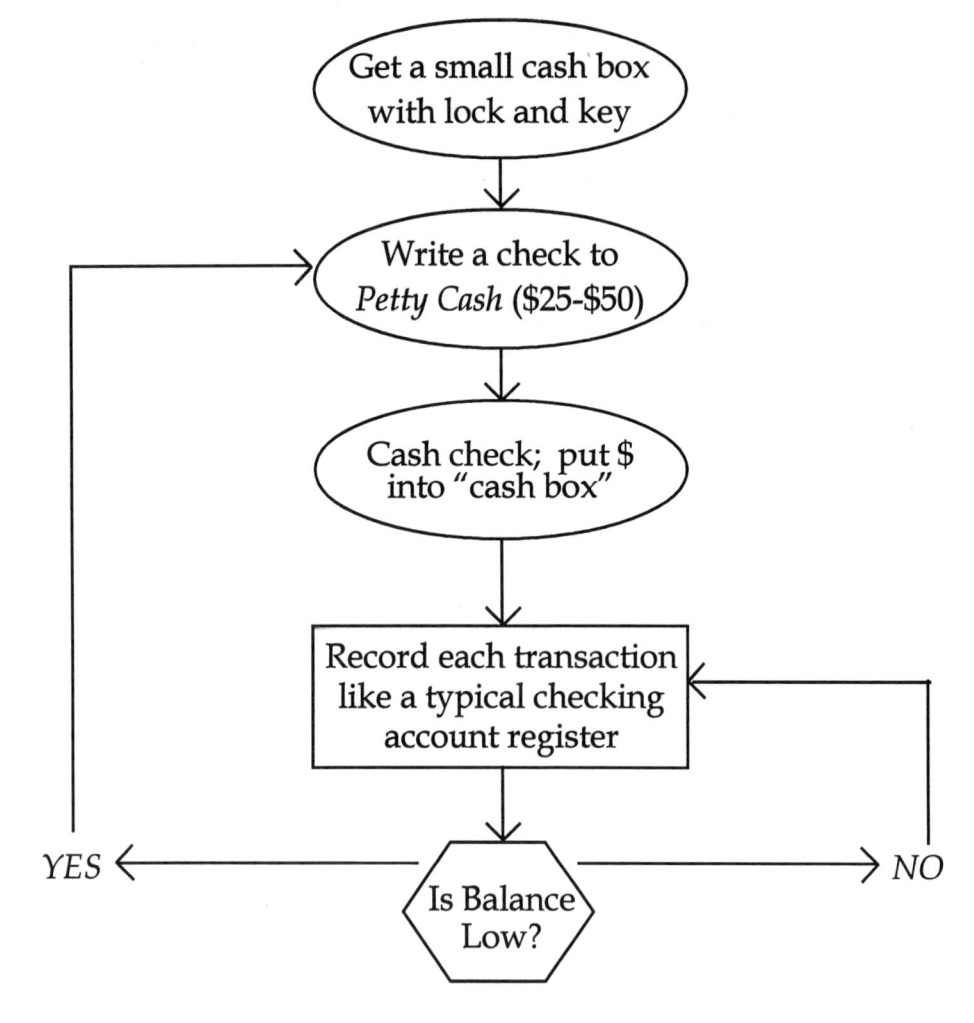

```
        ┌─────────────────────┐
        │ Get a small cash box│
        │  with lock and key  │
        └─────────┬───────────┘
                  ↓
        ┌─────────────────────┐
        │   Write a check to  │
 ┌─────→│ Petty Cash ($25-$50)│
 │      └─────────┬───────────┘
 │                ↓
 │      ┌─────────────────────┐
 │      │  Cash check; put $  │
 │      │   into "cash box"   │
 │      └─────────┬───────────┘
 │                ↓
 │      ┌─────────────────────┐
 │      │Record each transaction│←──┐
 │      │ like a typical checking│  │
 │      │   account register   │   │
 │      └─────────┬───────────┘   │
 │                ↓                │
 │          ╱ Is Balance ╲         │
 YES ←─────⟨    Low?     ⟩────→ NO┘
            ╲            ╱
```

I like to keep between $25 and $50 in petty cash. These denominations seem to be just the right amount for my petty cash expenditures.

Step 2: Identify Your Recordkeeping Needs

PETTY CASH RECORD
Company: Dakota ConsultingDate: 09/30/98

Date	Transaction	Expense Account	Deposits	Expenses	Balance
	Balance forward	===============	======	======>	$2.50
09/03/98	Deposit (Chk #531)		$50.00		$52.50
09/11/98	The Office Store	office supplies		$(3.10)	$49.40
09/14/98	Tea Connection	meals/entertainment		$(6.85)	$42.55
09/22/98	CSA Incorporated	postage		$(.78)	$41.77
09/23/98	Mart-Wall	office supplies		$(1.84)	$39.93
09/26/98	Margaret Queen	miscellaneous		$(2.10)	$37.83
09/29/98	USPS	postage		$(1.84)	$35.99

Figure 3 - Sample Petty Cash Record

I record all my petty cash transactions on my income and expense records. Also, if I take money from petty cash, I always replace it with a receipt or voucher to justify the expense.

These transactions should be recorded on your expense summary at the end of the month, quarter or year. But, you'll be reminded of this again in Step 5 - Generate Reports.

EXERCISE 4: *Tracking Your Fixed Assets for Depreciation.*

Fixed assets are the resources owned by a business but not used for resale. This exercise requires that you identify your fixed assets and determine their depreciation. Depreciation is an annual deduction that allows you to incrementally recover the cost of your business property. Incrementally means that you can deduct the cost of property over it's useful life (which is a predetermined number of years).

The basic requirements for depreciable business are:
1. It must be used in business or for the production of income.
2. It must have a determinable useful life that is longer than one year.
3. It must be something that wears, decays, gets used and loses value over time from natural causes.

There are also requirements that determine if your property cannot be depreciated. If the property meets these basic requirements, then you cannot depreciate it as a business expense:
1. It was disposed of in the same year as it was put into use.
2. It is used as part of inventory.
3. Repairs and replacements to the property increase it's useful life.

Examples of fixed assets that can be depreciated include furniture, vehicles, office equipment, buildings and proprietary rights (like copyrights and patents). Things you cannot depreciate include land, rental property (unless it is an income-producing property), repair costs that do not increase property value, inventory and items for resale.

To find out more on depreciating property and depreciation methods, please refer to IRS Publications #946 - *How to Depreciate Property* and #534 - *Depreciating Property Place in Service Before 1987.*

FIXED ASSET RECORD
Company: Dakota Consulting Date: 09/30/98

Asset	DOS*	Cost	% for Business	Recovery Period	Dep. Meth.**	Prev. Dep.***	Date Sold	Sale Price
Computer	03/02/98	$1,500.00	90%	5 year	200 DB	=====	N/A	N/A
Printer	03/02/98	$445.00	90%	5 year	200 DB	=====	N/A	N/A
Scanner	03/02/98	$399.00	90%	5 year	200 DB	=====	N/A	N/A
Fax	08/20/98	$329.00	100%	5 year	200 DB	=====	N/A	N/A
Bookshelf	09/01/98	$188.00	80%	7 year	200 DB	=====	N/A	N/A
Ergo chair	09/11/98	$275.00	100%	7 year	200 DB	=====	N/A	N/A
Desk	09/11/98	$350.00	100%	7 year	200 DB	====	N/A	N/A

* Date property was placed in service
** Depreciation method
*** Amount of depreciation previous allowed

Figure 4 - Sample Fixed Asset Record

Fixed assets cannot be deducted under an expense category. That's a double deduction!

EXERCISE 5: *Keeping Track of Accounts Receivable.*

You always need to keep track of who owes you money (its one of the reasons for being in business, isn't it?). An accounts receivable record (see Figure 5) is the answer. Accounts receivable helps you organize invoices for clients. Each client that has an open account with you (i.e., that client still owes you money for services you already performed for them) will have a detailed accounts receivable record entry.

Another purpose of accounts receivable is to track which clients have been naughty, and which clients have been nice. As your business grows, you may have the luxury of discontinuing service for those clients that consistently pay late. If your business deals in cash sales and you receive money at the same time of each transaction, you won't need to keep an accounts receivable record.

Since we are using the cash accounting method, we cannot record our income until we have received it.

ACCOUNTS RECEIVABLE RECORD

Company: Dakota Consulting   Date: 09/30/98

Invoice Date	Invoice Number	Amount Due	Terms	Date Paid	Amount Paid	Balance
08/20/98	0001025	$225.00	Net 15/10%	09/04/98	$206.75	$0.00
08/01/98	0001020	$115.00	Net 15/10%	08/31/98	$126.50	$18.25
06/24/98	0001018	$67.50	Net 15/10%	08/03/98	$74.25	$6.75
06/13/98	0001012	$121.50	Net 15/10%	06/30/98	$121.50	$0.00
06/01/98	0001011	$200.00	Net 15/10%	06/12/98	$200.00	$0.00
05/28/98	0001008	$300.00	Net 15/10%	06/02/98	$300.00	$0.00
05/17/98	0001001	$178.00	Net 15/10%	06/02/98	$178.00	$0.00

Figure 5 - Sample Accounts Receivable Record

Step 2: Identify Your Recordkeeping Needs

EXERCISE 6: Keeping Track of Accounts Payable.

Business owners often overlook their accounts payable because if you're like most, you hate to owe people money. But it's one of the necessary evils of doing business. The more diligent you are about keeping track of those vendors or creditors you owe money, the easier it will be to plan to pay them. This worksheet proves extremely helpful for those bills that you pay monthly, quarterly, or yearly. Note that, as in the case of accounts receivable, you'll have an accounts payable record for each vendor you do business with.

ACCOUNTS PAYABLE RECORD

Company: Dakota Consulting   Date: 09/30/98

Invoice Date	Invoice Number	Amount Due	Terms	Date Paid	Amount Paid	Balance
09/15/98	78-0148	$27.50	Net 30	***	$0.00	$55.00
08/15/98	78-0104	$27.50	Net 30	***	$0.00	$27.50
07/15/98	78-0090	$27.50	Net 30	08/04/98	$27.50	$0.00
06/15/98	78-0081	$27.50	Net 30	07/06/98	$27.50	$0.00
05/15/98	78-0065	$25.00	Net 30	06/02/98	$25.00	$0.00
04/15/98	78-0058	$25.00	Net 30	05/01/98	$25.00	$0.00
03/15/98	78-0054	$25.00	Net 30	04/02/98	$25.00	$0.00

Figure 6 - Sample Accounts Payable Record

You are an accounts receivable to those vendors or creditors with whom you do business!

EXERCISE 7: *Tracking transportation expenses.*

If you use a car for your business, you are eligible to deduct your business automobile expenses. To be eligible for transportation deductions you must know how much of your car is used for business. You also have to have extremely thorough records for this expense. There are several log books available to keep track of your usage, or you can use a worksheet like the one shown in Figure 7. Make sure you are realistic and exact about the percentage use of your car. To deduct 100% of your car for business is generally a rare occurrence, and is often considered a red flag to the IRS. It is imperative that you do not estimate this percentage. You will need to show total miles placed on your car as well as total miles used for business.

When using a car for transportation related to business, you may deduct the expense in one of two ways:

1. **Actual expense**: Tracking all expenses related to your mode of transportation to include gas, oil, tolls, parking, lease or rentals, car depreciation, repairs, licenses, insurance and registrations.

2. **Standard mileage rate:** This is a specific rate per mile that you use to deduct for business use of your car (the current rate for 1998 is 32.5 cents per mile).

Since the theme of this workbook is simplicity, the sample shown in Figure 7 uses the standard mileage rate for tracking transportation expenses.

> *You may want to calculate your mileage using both methods. Your deduction may not come out to the same value.*

TRANSPORTATION RECORD

Company: Dakota Consulting   Date: 09/30/98

Date	Destination	Client/Vendor	Purpose of Trip	Miles	Expense Amount
09/01/98	Longmont, CO	B&B Corporation	Consultation	37	$12.03
09/06/98	Greeley, CO	Insight	Consultation	42	$13.65
09/22/98	Loveland, CO	Print It	P/U presentation material	21	$6.83
09/26/98	Laramie, WY	University of Wyoming	Seminar presentation	48	$15.60
09/28/98	Boulder, CO	Murphy Law Associates	Consultation	42	$13.65

Figure 7 - Sample Transportation Record

Check with IRS Publications 334 – Tax Guide for Small Business and 917 – Business Use of Your Car for additional information.

Recordkeeping tips for tracking business miles

- January 1 - record the odometer reading
- Write the beginning and ending odometer reading for each business trip. The alternative is to just record the total miles for the business trip.
- Write in your day planner, the number of miles driven for the day for business.
- If you use the same route regularly, measure the distance of that route and multiply the miles by how many times you used that route for the year.
- If you use your car primarily for business (say 80%-90%), keep track of your personal miles and then subtract that at the end of the year to determine your business mileage.

EXERCISE 8: Tracking Travel Expenses.

Travel expenses are incurred while traveling away from home for business. IRS Publication #463 – *Travel, Entertainment, Gift and Car Expenses* lists and describes which travel expenses are valid. Some of those items that can be deducted while traveling for business include:

- transportation
- baggage & shipping
- lodging and meals
- telephone
- taxi, commuter bus & limousine
- car or truck
- cleaning expenses
- tips

While travel expenses are 100% deductible, meals while traveling are only 50% deductible. Don't worry, you will be creating a separate record for meals and entertainment (in the next exercise) to keep track of those expenses. Getting back to travel expenses, we are only going to discuss travel inside the U.S. Remember, the workbook theme is simplicity! Travel expense deductions are another red flag to the IRS, so be sure your records correctly reflect your activities.

Figure 8 shows a sample travel record kept by a Dakota Consulting representative for travel to a consultants convention.

If you intend on making part of your travels personal, make sure you keep the part specifically for business separate from those for personal. The personal part will not be deductible.

"Traveling is one way to lengthening life, at least in appearance."
— Benjamin Franklin

TRAVEL RECORD

Company: Dakota Consulting Dates: 09/09/98 to 09/13/98
Destination: Beaver Creek, CO Duration: 4 days
Purpose of Trip: Consulting Convention

Date	Location	Transaction	Meals*	Hotel	Taxis,etc.	Auto**	Misc.
09/09/98	Fort Collins	Rentals R Us			$31.50		
09/09/98	Idaho Springs	Cracker Barrel	$11.75 L				
09/09/98	Beaver Creek	Justin's	$13.75 D				
09/09/98	Beaver Creek	Holiday Inn		$52.00			
09/10/98	Beaver Creek	Holiday Inn		$52.00	$31.50		
09/11/98	Beaver Creek	Holiday Inn		$52.00	$31.50		
09/12/98	Beaver Creek	Holiday Inn		$52.00	$31.50		
09/13/98	Beaver Creek	Holiday Inn	$8.50 B				
09/13/98	Evergreen	Wendy's	$5.25 L				
09/13/98	Fort Collins	Rentals R Us			$31.50		

* B, L, D = Breakfast, Lunch, Dinner respectively
** G, P, T - Gas, Parking, Tolls respectively

Figure 8 - Sample Travel Record

***EXERCISE 9:** Tracking Meals and Entertainment Expenses.*

If you entertain clients for business purposes, then you may be able to deduct this expense. Once again, you must keep accurate and thorough records to justify the expense. So that this "privilege" is not misused, you may be asked to show that your expenses are directly related to business activity.

Meals and entertainment expenses are yet another potential red flag to the IRS. This is mainly because people tend to slack off while keeping records. The IRS lets you deduct two types of meals:
1. Meals eaten away from home on an overnight business trip; and
2. Meals eaten while conducting activities that are a benefit for your business.

Examples of activities that would be to the benefit of your business include: meeting with a potential client, meeting with a person giving you a referral, meeting an existing client, and meeting with colleagues to discuss aspects of the business.

In addition to recording the purpose of your meeting, you may want to record (in your day planner) topics that were discussed. This just gives you better amunition in the event you need to explain or justify the expense.

The IRS will only let you deduct 50% of your business-related meals and entertainment costs.

Step 2: Identify Your Recordkeeping Needs

MEALS & ENTERTAINMENT RECORD
Company: Dakota Consulting   Date: 09/01/98 thru 09/30/98

Date	Location	Purpose	Entertainee	Amount
09/07/98	Jackson's Hole Eatery	Consulting	Insight	$38.20
09/12/98	Austins	Consulting	RC Communications	$28.37
09/26/98	MacRonalds	Seminar Break	University of Wyoming	$12.50
09/28/98	The Broker	Consulting	Murphy Law Associates	$54.11
09/29/98	Gibster Bagel Shop	Project delivery	Margaret Queen	$7.90
09/30/98	Austins	Initial meeting	Technology Experts	$31.86

Figure 9 - Sample Meals & Entertainment Record

For a summary of the rules regarding entertainment expenses, reference IRS Publication #334 – *Tax Guide for Small Business*. There is a table in section 8 of the publication that walks you through rules and tests to determine appropriate deductions.

EXERCISE 10: Determining Your Net Worth.

This is a snapshot of your assets and liabilities. You want to list all of your assets (the fun part) and all of your liabilities (the not-so-fun part) . This exercise will help you determine the equity of your business. For more advanced recordkeeping, which you may choose to do in the future, this statement will help you track the financial efficacy of your business and allow you to make appropriate modifications. Financial efficacy is just a fancy phrase meaning the effectiveness or intended results of your business' recordkeeping operations.

In order to calculate your net worth, you must first complete a balance sheet like the sample shown in Figure 10. The balance sheet is a worksheet used to identify your assets and liabilities. Net worth is equal to your assets minus your liabilities. Take a few moments to fill out a balance sheet and determine your net worth. A sample is provided for you to use as a guideline, but yes, you actually have to do the work yourself for your own business!

One benefit of using accounting software becomes apparent in this exercise. Imagine preparing a balance sheet by hand every time. Tedious, wouldn't you agree? Accounting software automatically generates a periodic balance sheet for you based on the accounts that are already established.

All of the records you have created up to this point will come in handy while filling out your balance sheet — make sure you have them nearby!

Step 2: Identify Your Recordkeeping Needs

Dakota Consulting Company
Balance Sheet
September 30, 1998

ASSETS

 Current Assets

  Cash on Hand $50.00

  Petty Cash $37.85

  Accounts Receiveable $574.95

  Short-term Investments $0.00

 Long-term Investments $2,500.00

 Fixed Assets

  Equipment (computer, printer, scanner, fax) $2,673.00

  Furniture   (bookshelf, chair, desk) $813.00

           TOTAL ASSETS $6,648.80

LIABILITIES

 Current Liabilities

  Accounts Payable $85.90

  Interest Payable $67.89

  Taxes Payable

   Federal $0.00

   Self-employment $110.00

   State $125.00

 Long-term Liabilities (Loan) $2,000.00

          TOTAL LIABILITES $2,388.79

NET WORTH = $4,260.01

Figure 10 - Sample Balance Sheet

Now that you've experimented with these basic recordkeeping skills, it is time to go on to the next step. But, if you're feeling overwhelmed at this point, review Step 2 again. Practice with the forms in Appendix A until you feel more comfortable moving on to Step 3.

Let's take a look at what we have accomplished so far. We have:

1. Identified your tax calendar;

2. Identified your accounting method;

3. Set up income and expense records;

4. Set up a petty cash record;

5. Determined your fixed assets;

6. Set up an accounts receivable record;

7. Set up an accounts payable record;

8. Set up travel, transportation and entertainment records;

9. Generated a preliminary balance sheet; and

10. Determined your net worth.

Congratulations! You have identified and organized your primary recordkeeping needs.

STEP 3
Compile Client and Vendor Records

STEP 3 ACTIVITIES:
- Organize a client database
- Identify the benefits of a client database
- Organize a vendor database
- Identify the benefits of a vendor database

Step 3: Compile Client and Vendor Records

O.K. Take a breather. You've just compiled most of the records you will need for your business. You deserve a break! This workbook and Step 3 will be here when you get back.

« « BREAK » »

Are you ready? Great! We're about to compile client and vendor records. These two records are fairly straightforward, but if you're like me, you'll have lots of them. Clients are what makes your business the success that it is; vendors help you serve those clients.

Let's start with client records. It's never too late to compile a database of existing and prospective clients. This can be done either by hand or you can be a brave adventurer, and try one of the sophisticated database software packages. Compiling this record allows you to keep track of the different types of clients you serve. It will provide the information you need to analyze your customer base. This in turn can help you make better decisions regarding marketing and advertising strategies for your business.

> **Example:** After compiling your client records you may discover that a large portion of your clients reside in the same locality. This information can be used to focus your marketing plan and save on advertising expenses.

Figure 11 shows a sample of the information you should retain. You may want to organize these on 3 x 5 index cards and keep them in an index card file. Alternatively, you may collect this information in a spreadsheet program (e.g., Excel or QuattroPro) or database program (e.g., AlphaFive or Paradox).

> **JUSTIN CASE**   Account No. dc-0001
>
> Address: 9994 Starship Drive
>   Enterprise, CO 11189
>
> Home Phone: (970) 555-1234   Work Phone: (970) 555-4400
> Fax: (970) 555-4401   E-mail: jcstar@aol.com
>
> *SERVICES PROVIDED:*
> 1. Seminar preparation
> 2. Technical writing of company procedures
>
> *ADDITIONAL NOTES:*
> Justin plays golf every Friday at 1 p.m.
> Wife - Sarah; daughter - Jessica

Figure 11 - Sample Client Information

The main benefits of keeping client records include:
1. Better client retention;
2. Better repeat service;
3. Increase referral potential; and
4. Better service to your clients.

As a service-oriented business, client base, repeat service and referrals are the foundation of a successful and continued business. It will be up to you to determine how much information is necessary per client. Whatever method you choose to compile this information, remember a client database is a key factor in the survival of your business.

Step 3: Compile Client and Vendor Records

We often forget that vendors, like our clients, are an integral part of our business. Even though you are a service-oriented business, you still rely on vendors to provide you with the necessary supplies to help operate your business. Types of vendors include those places where you get office supplies, furniture, computer supplies and the like.

Services that you rely on are also vendors. These may include on-line services, phone companies and utility companies. I find it convenient to keep information on the vendors that I patronize frequently. The example shown in Figure 12 gives you an idea of what information may be needed for those frequently-used vendors.

O. VERMILLION　　　　　　　　　　　　　Account No. dc-v-0001

Contact:　　James Right
Address:　　1100 Northstart Lane
　　　　　　Enterprise, CO 11189

Phone:　　　(970) 555-9980
Fax:　　　　(970) 555-1112
Email:　　　　　overmillion@servicecorp.com

PROVIDES:
general office supplies, furniture, books, software, computers and peripherals

ADDITIONAL NOTES:
Opened account on:　　03/01/98　Acct#:　　　624881
Discount provided on bulk purchases
Terms of payment: Net 30 days

Figure 12 - Sample Vendor Information

A vendor database facilitates the tracking of your business' lifeline – the supplies and incidentals that keep your business running. You can also use your vendor records to determine where to cut costs and save money.

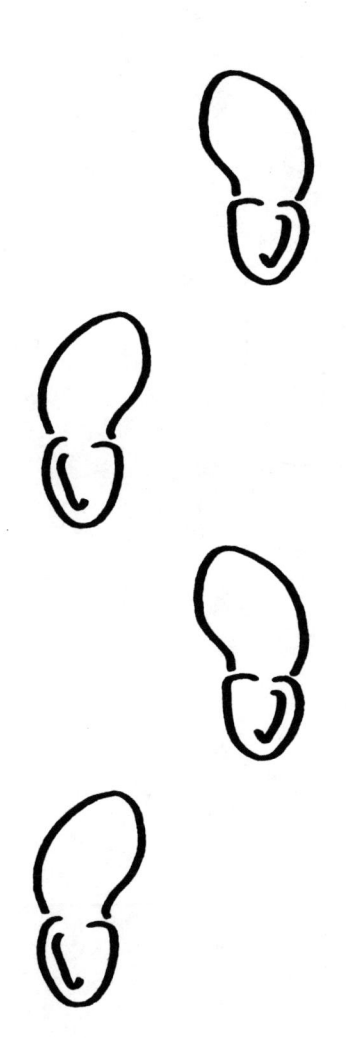

STEP 4
Create a Service List

STEP 4 ACTIVITIES:
- Identify services provided to clients
- Create a comprehensive service list

Step 4: Create a Service List

You run a service-oriented business (otherwise you wouldn't be this far into the book!), but what exactly is it that you provide? Whether your particular service is consulting, desktop publishing or physical therapy you need a service list! This service list should be reassessed on a regular basis, because rates change and your services will change. The list should contain at least the following information: item or category that the service falls under, a description of the service and price charged for each service.

Maintaining a service list allows you to track which particular services are productive for your business and which ones are not. This list should be used in conjunction with your income record to determine which services to keep and which services to re-evaluate due to unprofitability.

A service list also provides a handy reference for those situations in which you answer phone calls about your business. The example shown in Figure 13 gives you an idea of what kind of services Dakota Consulting provides to its clients and the corresponding rates.

As short as this step may seem on paper, it is actually an important part of your business success. Do not overlook this step because of its size! Use your service list as a tool to track trends. As mentioned earlier, periodically review your services and your income summary. These two items together will reveal alot about the strength or weakness of the service or services you provide to your clients.

"It is not where you serve, but how you serve."

— J. Rubin Clark

Service Item/Category	Service Description	Rate
Consultation: Initial	Initial client consultation	$25 per hour
Consultation: FUP	Followup consultation	$10 flat rate
Seminar: Prep	Seminar preparation	$20 per hour
Seminar: Conduct	Conduct seminar	$75-$100 per person
Writing: Technical	Technical writing service	$20 per hour
Writing: Advertising	Advertisement writing service	$25 per hour

Figure 13 - Sample Service List

Keep a copy of your service list by the phone to assist you when a new potential client calls with questions about your business and services!

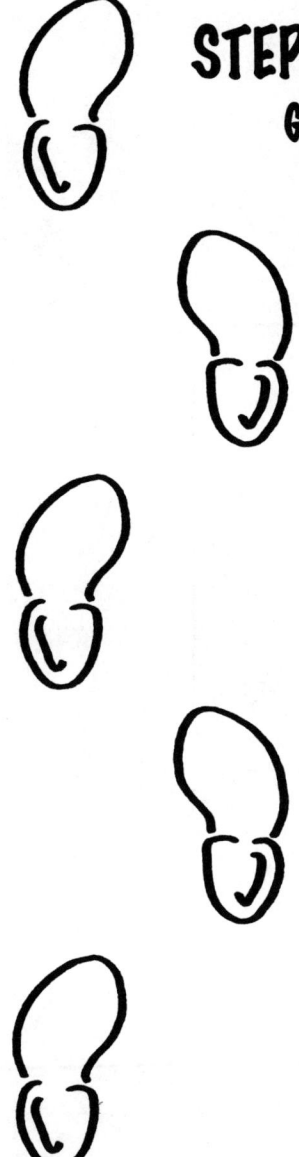

STEP FIVE
Generate Reports

STEP 5 ACTIVITIES:
- Determine report generation period
- Generate income summary
- Generate expense summary
- Generate another balance sheet
- Generate profit and loss statement
- Establish a sample recordkeeping schedule

Step 5: Generate Reports

Now that you've gathered all this information about your business, what do you do with all of it? Good question. You need to report it. You will first need to decide what kind of reports to generate with all of these data. Then you will want to determine your report generation period (i.e., monthly, quarterly, yearly). Whichever period you choose, make sure you are consistent.

I generate my reports quarterly because it corresponds with the IRS tax calendars and tax requirements for sole proprietors.

It's best to get it all organized before the tax deadline. By now you should have established a system of recordkeeping that works well for you and corresponds well with the tax schedule for sole proprietors. This step involves a lot of tabulation, so be patient and stick with it. And just think, once you're done with Step 5, you'll only have one more step to go!

The summaries presented here in Step 5 will help you determine the financial efficacy of your business. They will show trends such as: high and low income periods, effective advertising periods, high expense times and much more. Make use of these tools. They can help you make appropriate decisions to strengthen your business. If you're not sure what some of the trends mean, seek out a professional to help you clarify them.

Don't give up now, you're almost there!

"Organizing is what you do before you do something, so that when you do it, it's not all mixed up."

— A.A. Milne

Income Summary: A report of all entries from your income record (from Step 2) for a given time period. The sample shown below was generated for the entire year of 1998, but is broken down by quarter. Note that the sample in Figure 14 summarizes income by services.

I like to use this type of summary so I don't have to regenerate a new worksheet for each quarter. It's all summarized on one sheet at the end of the year.

Income (services)	QTR1	QTR2	QTR3	QTR4	TOTAL
Consultation:Initial	$625.51	$885.24	$250.78	$1,875.34	$3,636.87
Consultation: Follow up	$105.07	$264.28	$130.97	$540.16	$1,040.48
Seminar: Preparation	$287.15	$123.87	$557.68	$1,201.98	$2,170.68
Seminar: Conduct	$875.00	$232.75	$215.95	$1,575.75	$2,899.45
Writing: Technical	$125.00	$162.45	$188.75	$120.15	$596.35
Writing: Advertising	$150.25	$117.88	$212.00	$210.55	$690.68
TOTAL	$2,167.98	$1,786.47	$1,556.13	$5,523.93	$11,0345.51

Figure 14 - Sample Income Summary

By examining this summary you can begin to see certain trends about your income. From the sample shown above, Dakota Consulting makes most of their income from initial consultations and seminars. This information can help you identify potentially weak areas (in this case, follow up consultations and writing).

Step 5: Generate Reports

Expense Summary: A report of all entries from your expense record for a given time period. The expense summary shown in Figure 15 is broken down by quarters, but is filled in for the entire year of 1998. The summary requires that you list all of the expense categories and the amount associated with the each.

Expense	QTR1	QTR2	QTR3	QTR4	TOTAL
Advertising	$125.75	$125.75	$215.85	$125.75	$593.10
Postage & Handling	$56.78	$62.75	$67.33	$50.18	$237.04
Office Supplies	$82.73	$154.74	$144.25	$187.43	$569.15
Utilities	$151.00	$147.89	$150.77	$148.75	$598.41
Professional Development	$25.00	$57.29	$90.00	$149.00	$321.29
Miscellaneous	$191.13	$91.75	$82.84	$122.33	$488.05
TOTAL	$632.39	$640.17	$751.04	$783.44	$2,807.04

Figure 15 - Sample Expense Summary

One significant trend seen in this summary is in advertising. Dakota Consulting spent more money on advertising in the third quarter than any other quarter. Information like this can help your business budget expenses for the next year.

As mentioned earlier, if you aren't sure what type of trends are appearing or what they mean, be sure to solicit help from a knowledgeable source. Understanding these trends puts you in the position to make better decisions about your business.

The following summaries, the balance sheet and the profit and loss statement, are the two parts that make up your financial statement. These two reports provide key information in determining the status of your business. The balance sheet is the first part of the financial statement. It lists your assets and liabilities at a specific date in time (basically a snapshot of your business worth) and is used to determine your net worth or equity. The profit and loss statement is the second part of the financial statement and is generated for a certain span of time (usually for the month or quarter).

Balance Sheet: You completed a preliminary Balance Sheet in Exercise 7 of Step 2, but for accuracy, complete a final Balance Sheet to incorporate into your report generation section. You can photocopy the one you've already done and place it with the rest of these reports.

Profit and Loss Statement: A summary of all business income and expenses for a certain time period (i.e., month, quarter, year). Also referred to as an income statement or operating statement. The profit and loss statement (*see* Figure 16) is different from the balance sheet in that it provides a constant picture of your business activity over the course of a given time period. Remember, the balance sheet was just a snapshot of your business at a specific time.

I prepare a profit and loss statement at the close of each month using the information from my expense and income records.

" In the end we retain from our studies only that which we practically apply."
— Johann Wolfgang Von Goethe

Step 5: Generate Reports

Dakota Consulting Company
Profit and Loss Statement
July 1 - September 30, 1998

INCOME
    Fees $350.00
    Services $3,689.00

TOTAL INCOME $4,039.00

EXPENSES

Advertising	$549.00
Bank Charges	$9.00
Dues & Subscriptions	$59.85
Equipment Rental	$29.85
Licenses & Permits	$15.00
Postage and Handling	$112.50
Office Supplies	$108.23
Telephone	$168.75

TOTAL EXPENSES $1,052.18

NET PROFIT (Income - Expenses) = $2,986.82

Figure 16 - Sample Profit and Loss Statement

"Where profit is, loss is hidden near by."

— Japanese Proverb

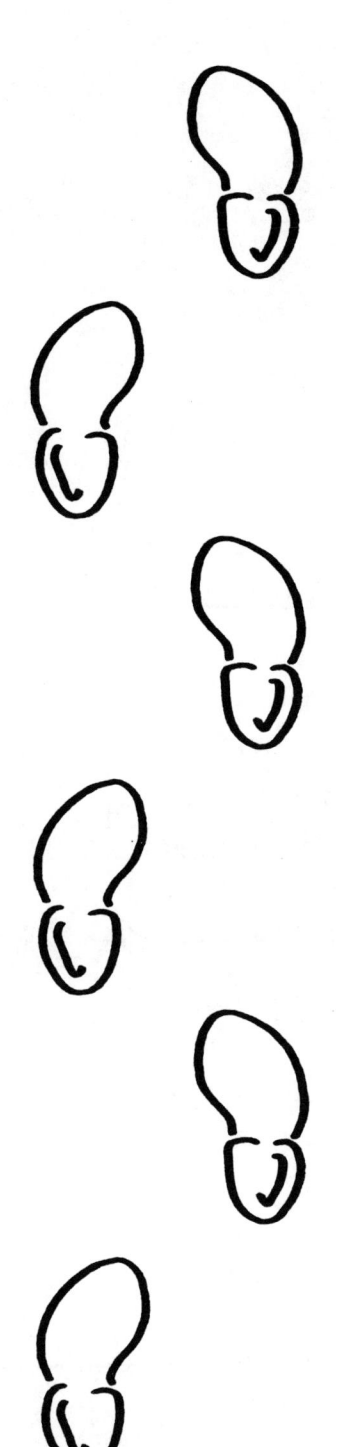

STEP SIX
Keep the IRS Happy

STEP 6 ACTIVITES:
- Identify basic IRS forms for the sole proprietor
- Understand the purpose of each schedule or form
- Review a typical tax schedule for the sole proprietor

Step 6: Keep the IRS Happy

Remember, you should be as dedicated to the IRS as you are to your own business, so take the time to check your legalities. This is a good time to rely on your readily available resources for tax preparation and small business accounting. The IRS provides several *free* publications to help you in this process. Publication #334 – *Tax Guide for Small Business,* should certainly be part of your business library.

The better you understand this tax preparation process, the happier you will make the IRS and yourself. Be sure to review and understand the primary forms you will use for your business. Most of the tax forms that you are responsible for are listed and briefly discussed below. Sample forms and schedules are shown in Appendix D – IRS Tax Forms.

Keep in mind that every business is unique and depending on your business scenario, you may need other forms.

Schedule C/C-EZ, Profit or (Loss) from Business or Profession

This is a required tax form for all sole proprietors. All of your income and expenses will be listed on this form. It shouldn't be that foreign to you since you've already generated a profit and loss report in Step 5. Schedule C is analogous to a profit and loss statement for the tax year.

Schedule SE, Computation of Social Security Self-Employment Tax

If you earn income from self-employment, this form will assist you in determining your social security and medicare taxes. These taxes should be paid as part of your estimated quarterly tax (Form 1040–ES).

Form 1040-ES, Estimated Tax for Sole Proprietors

You will need to complete this form if your income is not subject to withholdings. This process requires you to make quarterly estimated tax payments. Remember the suggestion to open a business savings account from the *Preliminary Business Preparations* checklist? That money set aside can be used to send in with this form.

Form 4562, Depreciation and Amortization

Remember the fixed assets record you prepared back in Step 2? Here is where that record will come in handy for tax preparation. You will calculate the annual deduction to recover from your investments listed in your fixed assets log using Form 4562.

Form 8829, Expenses for Business Use of Your Home

This form is used by the sole proprietor to deduct that part of their home that they *strictly* use for business. Make sure you understand the rules, they are very stringent. If you do not work out of your home, this form is not necessary.

Please *do not* accept this chapter as an authoritative source for your tax preparation. Do your research and make sure you've covered all the bases. The IRS will greatly appreciate it and you will save yourself many headaches down the road. Figure 17 shows a basic tax calendar for the sole proprietor service-oriented business, using the cash accounting method. This calendar lists specific dates in which the sole proprietor is responsible for certain tax requirements. IRS Publication #509 – *Tax Calendars* gives a comprehensive summary of the tax calendars for all business structures to include the sole proprietor. There are many free IRS publications (*see* Appendix C – Suggested IRS Publications) to help you answer most of your tax questions.

Step 6: Keep the IRS Happy

Calendar Date	Tax Item	Schedule/Form to Use
January 15	Estimated tax	Form 1040-ES
April 15	Income tax	Form 1040/Schedule C
April 15	Self-employment tax	Form 1040/Schedule SE
April 15	Estimated tax	Form 1040-ES
June 15	Estimated tax	Form 1040-ES
September 15	Estimated tax	Form 1040-ES

Figure 17 - Sample Tax Schedule for the Sole Proprietor

Pat yourself on the back! You're finished! You've made it!

Now that you have worked through this six step process, you should feel more confident about your business recordkeeping. I realize that the "by-hand" method is tedious, time consuming and almost archaic, but you are a more knowledgeable sole proprietor as a result! You also have this workbook as a reference if you ever need to re-work your books. Thanks for hanging tough!

"The reward of a thing well done is to have done it."

— Ralph Waldo Emerson

Let's Recheck Our Steps!

STEP 1: Understand the Purpose of Your Books.

You should know the two primary reasons for keeping your books: for tracking your business performance and for tax preparation. We also looked at other important reasons to keep records. You should also know the difference between the single entry and double entry accounting systems. But don't just *know* the difference; make sure you understand how both systems work.

STEP 2: Identify Your Recordkeeping Needs.

You created many records in this step and answered a few key questions. You came out of this step knowing which tax calendar you are using, which accounting method you will use (cash vs. accrual) and what information goes into each record. You now have the following records: income, expense, fixed assets, petty cash, travel, transportation, meals & entertainment and a balance sheet.

STEP 3: Compile Client and Vendor Records.

This step made you more aware of the importance of keeping client and vendor records. The maintenance of these records can be a key factor in the success of your business and building a strong client-customer relationship.

STEP 4: Create a Service List.

Your list of services should now be in a format conducive to running your business efficiently. Your brainstorming should have created a masterpiece of a list. Of course, this step requires maintenance and updating, but you've already done it, so each update should be a breeze!

STEP 5: Generate Reports.

You may have struggled with this step because it required a lot of time and tabulations. But if you stuck with it and continued through to the end, you came through this step with some important financial records. From this step, you created some period summary reports, a balance sheet and profit and loss statement.

STEP 6: Keep the IRS Happy.

Keeping the IRS happy is as important as keeping your business productive. This step showed you many of the necessary forms to use for tax preparation. It also referred you to important sources for tax information. Be sure to use these resources. There's no need to voluntarily throw red flags at the IRS!

"I never stop to plan. I take things step by step."
— Mary McLeod Bethune

Recordkeeping Troubleshooting

If you have been diligent following the six steps of this workbook, your business records are now in order. Let's look at some common issues that often come up in recordkeeping. You may have encountered some of these along the way.

1. How do I know if my records are adequate?

Adequate records means that you have written or oral proof to substantiate your business expenses and income. Using the term "adequate" is somewhat subjective. However, you are keeping an adequate set of records if: you have a diary or log of your expenses; you have documentary evidence (i.e., receipts, paid bills, etc.); and your business expenses can be recreated based on the facts of the circumstances.

2. How should I record credit card purchases?

They should be treated just like a normal expenses. It would probably be easier to create a credit card payable record. Then, you write a check from your business checking account to either the credit card or to your personal account.

If your business requires the use of a credit card, you may want to have a separate business credit card. You should then create a credit card record similar to your expense record for the convenience of tracking business costs.

3. How do I deduct the interest from my credit card?

You can deduct 100% of your credit card interest if that card has been used solely for business. If you have been using the credit card for both personal and business purposes, you will have to determine how much was used for business and use that percentage as your interest deduction.

4. How do I determine under which tax categories to group my expenses?

IRS Publication #334 – *Tax Guide for Small Business* has a sample that shows common categories. Use this as a template to start with and then add or subtract to these categories. Also take a look at Part II – Expenses on a Schedule C form. This will also give you a good starting point.

5. Can I bill my clients using my recordkeeping information?

Yes. Billing your clients will be much easier now that you have records of accounts receivables and your client information file. Bill your clients using an invoice form. Many of today's word processing, spreadsheet and accounting software packages have invoice templates ready-made for this task. Number your invoice forms to provide a nice audit trail.

6. Can't I do all of this using today's accounting software?

Absolutely! But as I've suggested before, I would start out doing it manually first. I find that I understand things better and retain information longer if I get personally involved – you will too! After generating your records and reports by hand, experiment with some of the suggested accounting software listed in Appendix B – References & Resources.

Also, keep in mind that these accounting software packages are setup on the basis that the person entering the information is somewhat knowledgeable of the recordkeeping process. Remember, what you put into a computer is what you get out. So if you are not sure of the information to provide to these packages, make sure you get the proper assistance.

7. Where do I keep my records?

Keep current records in your office in a filing cabinet that is within arm's reach. Records from previous years should be organized such that you can go back to access them by the year. A safety precaution is to make copies of your records and keep them in a safe deposit box or fire proof safe.

8. How long should I keep my records?

For your federal tax return, the IRS has three years to look over your tax records. Therefore, at a minimum you should keep tax records and corresponding receipts for three years and in some cases up to seven years. The general rule of thumb is to hold onto your tax return and all associated items for three to five years from the date you filed the return or paid the tax, whichever occurs last.

For fixed assets, you should keep receipts for the time period that you own the property, plus three to five years.

9. Can I start recordkeeping from the current month or do I have to start from January?

First, as mentioned in Step 2, the tax calendar year is most appropriate for the sole proprietor service-oriented business. You can start from the current month if that is when you opened for business. For example, if you opened your business for operation in March, your calendar year will be from January until December. You just won't have any transactions to report for January and February.

Recordkeeping Troubleshooting

10. *What do I do with the transactions that were made from my personal account before I switched them over to my business account?*

Record them into your business account as you would a normal expense. It's a good idea to write "I Owe Yous" to yourself and store them in your petty cash box. Then at some designated time, you can write a lump sum check from your business account back to your personal account in the amount of your expenditures.

11. *Who should keep my records?*

You - If you are just starting a business and it is extremely simple (i.e., sole-proprietor, no employees, one location, minimal services, etc.) then you can generate and maintain your own records.

Bookkeeper or Accountant - If your records are still fairly simple, but you need assistance with tracking business trends and creating financial reports, a bookkeeper may be sufficient. As your business becomes more complex, you may require an accountant.

Bookkeeping or Accounting Service - This type of service compiles receipts, canceled checks and invoices. Then they will generate the necessary financial statements required for your business.

Computer - Use a computer as an enhancement to your current recordkeeping system. It cannot take the place of you or your bookkeeper or accountant, but it can be an extremely productive tool.

12. Which method of car deduction expense can I use for a leased car?
You can only use the standard mileage rate since this method accounts for depreciation of a car. You cannot depreciate property you don't own!

13. What should I do with all of the receipts kept for the year?
Your receipts should be stored away with all of the forms and reports you generated for that particular year. Remember the suggested three-ring binder from the *Recordkeeping Necessities Checklist*? This is where that will come in handy.

14. How many years can you report a loss and still continue normal business operations?
The Federal law says that you are in business if you show a profit for 3 out of 5 years. If this condition is not met, your business will be considered a hobby. As a result, you will not be eligible for tax deductions or a tax write-off from your business.

APPENDIX A
Worksheets

These blank forms are for your use. Feel free to make multiple copies. They make good practice sheets!

INCOME RECORD

COMPANY:
DATE:

REFERENCE	DATE	TRANSACTION	INCOME	TOTAL

Appendix A – Worksheets

EXPENSE RECORD

COMPANY: DATE:														
REFERENCE	DATE	TRANSACTION												

page ____ of ____

Record your own expense categories here

PETTY CASH RECORD

COMPANY:					
DATE:					

DATE	TRANSACTION	EXPENSE ACCOUNT	DEPOSITS	EXPENSES	BALANCE
	Balance Forward	============	======	=====>	

FIXED ASSET RECORD

COMPANY:
DATE:

page ___ of ___

ASSET	DOS*	COST	% FOR BUSINESS	RECOVERY PERIOD	DEP. METHOD**	PREVIOUS DEP***	DATE SOLD	SALE PRICE

*Date Placed in Service; ** Depreciation method; *** Amount of depreciation previously allowed

ACCOUNTS RECEIVABLE RECORD

COMPANY:
DATE:

INVOICE DATE	INVOICE NUMBER	AMOUNT DUE	TERMS	DATE PAID	AMOUNT PAID	BALANCE

Appendix A – Worksheets

ACCOUNTS PAYABLE RECORD

COMPANY:
DATE:

INVOICE DATE	INVOICE NUMBER	AMOUNT DUE	TERMS	DATE PAID	AMOUNT PAID	BALANCE

TRANSPORTATION RECORD

COMPANY:
DATE:

DATE	DESTINATION	CLIENT	PURPOSE OF TRIP	MILES	AMOUNT

Appendix A – Worksheets

TRAVEL RECORD

COMPANY: DESTINATION: PURPOSE OF TRIP:				DATES: to DURATION:			
DATE	LOCATION	TRANSACTION	MEALS	HOTEL	TAXIS, ETC.	AUTO	MISC

MEALS & ENTERTAINMENT RECORD

COMPANY:				
DATE:				

DATE	LOCATION	PURPOSE	ENTERTAINEE	AMOUNT

Appendix A – Worksheets

BALANCE SHEET

COMPANY: **DATE:**

ASSETS
    Current Assets
        Cash on Hand $ _____
        Petty Cash $ _____
        Accounts Receivable $ _____
        Short-term Investments $ _____
    Long-term Investments $ _____
    Fixed Assets
        Equipment $ _____
        Furniture $ _____

                TOTAL ASSETS $ _____

LIABILITIES
    Current Liabilities
        Accounts Payable $ _____
        Interest Payable $ _____
        Taxes Payable
            Federal $ _____
            Self-employment $ _____
            State $ _____
    Long-term Liabilities $ _____

                TOTAL LIABILITIES $ _____

NET WORTH (Total Assets - Total Liabilities) = $

SERVICE LIST

COMPANY:		
DATE:		

SERVICE ITEM/CATEGORY	SERVICE DESCRIPTION	SERVICE RATE

Appendix A – Worksheets

INCOME SUMMARY (MONTHLY)

COMPANY:
DATE:

Income (Services)	JAN	FEB	MAR	APR	MAY	JUN	JUL	AUG	SEP	OCT	NOV	DEC	TOTAL
TOTAL													

INCOME SUMMARY (QUARTERLY/ANNUALLY)

COMPANY:
DATE:

Income (Services)	QTR1	QTR2	QTR3	QTR4	TOTAL
TOTAL					

Appendix A – Worksheets

EXPENSE SUMMARY (MONTHLY)

COMPANY:
DATE:

Expense	JAN	FEB	MAR	APR	MAY	JUN	JUL	AUG	SEP	OCT	NOV	DEC	TOTAL
TOTAL													

EXPENSE SUMMARY (QUARTERLY/ANNUALLY)

COMPANY:
DATE:

Expense	QTR1	QTR2	QTR3	QTR4	TOTAL
TOTAL					

Appendix A – Worksheets

PROFIT AND LOSS STATEMENT

COMPANY:
REPORT GENERATED FOR:

INCOME

    Fees $ _____
    Services $ _____
                            TOTAL INCOME $ _____

EXPENSES

    Advertising $ _____
    Bank Charges $ _____
    Dues & Subscriptions $ _____
    Equipment Rental $ _____
    Licenses & Permits $ _____
    Postage & Handling $ _____
    Office Supplies $ _____
    Telephone $ _____
    _____ $ _____
    _____ $ _____
    _____ $ _____
    _____ $ _____
    _____ $ _____
                            TOTAL EXPENSES $ _____

NET PROFIT (Total Income - Total Expenses) = $ _____

APPENDIX B
References & Resources

•••Books•••

Many of the books listed here are part of my working library and others are ones that I have referenced or checked out of the library once or twice or three times. There is a broad range of books listed, but the majority deal with recordkeeping either briefly or in depth. Of course, I will continue to add to my personal library and you should as well. You can never have enough references and resources.

Bautista, Beltisezar B. *How to Build a Successful One-Person Business.* Farmington Hills, MI: Bookhaus Publisher, 1995.

Brabec, Barbara. *Homemade Money* (5th Edition). Cincinnati, OH: Betterway Books, 1994.

Broussard, Cheryl. *Sister CEO: The Black Woman's Guide to Starting Your Own Business.* Farmington, NY: Viking, 1997.

Broussard, Cheryl. *A Black Woman's Guide to Financial Independence: Smart Ways to Take Charge of Your Money, Build Wealth and Achieve Financial Security.* Farmington, NY: Viking, 1994.

Carter, Gary W. *Taxes Made Easy for Your Home-Based Business.* New York, NY: Macmillan Publishing, 1997.

Edwards, Paul & Sarah. *The Best Home Businesses for the 90s.* New York, NY: G.P. Putnam's Sons, 1994.

Fields, Louis. *Bookkeeping Made Simple.* New York, NY: DoubleDay, 1990.

Gelb, Joseph. *Tax Accounting for Small Business: How to prepare a 1040C.* Woodmere, NY: Small Business Advisor, 1996.

Kamoroff, Bernard. *Small-Time Operator.* Laytonville, CA: Bell Springs Publishing, 1995.

Kern, Coralee Smith and Tammara Hoffman Wolfgram. *How to Run Your Own Home Business*. Lincolnwood, IL: VGM Career Horizon, 1995.

Kravitz, Wallace W. *Bookkeeping the Easy Way*. Barrons Educational Services, 1990.

Lickson, Charles & Bryane. *Finances and Taxes for the Home-Based Business*. Menlo Park, CA: Crisp Publications, 1997.

Mose, Arlene K., Jackson, John and Gary Downs. *Day-to-Day Business Accounting*. Englewood Cliffs, NJ: Prentice Hall, 1997.

Pinson, Linda and Jerry Jinnett. *Anatomy of a Business Plan*. Chicago, IL: Upstart Publishing Company, 1996.

Pinson, Linda and Jerry Jinnett. *Keeping the Books* (3rd Edition). Chicago, IL: Upstart Publishing Company, 1996.

Pinson, Linda and Jerry Jinnett. *The Home-Based Entrepreneur* (2nd Edition). Dearborn, IL: Upstart Publishing Company, Inc., 1989.

Pinson, Linda and Jerry Jinnett. *Out of Your Mind...And Into the Marketplace*. Dover, NH: Upstart Publishing Company, 1988.

Ragan, Robert C. *Step-By-Step Bookkeeping* (Revised Edition). New York, NY: Sterling Publishing Co., Inc., 1992.

Sitarz, Daniel. *Small Business Accounting*. Carbondale, IL: Nova Publishing Company, 1995.

Tabet, Joseph and Jeffrey Slater. *Financial Essentials for Small Business Success*. Chicago, IL:Upstart Publishing Company, 1994.

Tyson, Eric and David J. Silverman. *Taxes for Dummies* (1998 Edition). Foster City, CA: IDG Books Worldwide, 1998.

Zobel, Jan. *Minding Her Own Business: The Self-Employed Woman's Guide to Taxes & Recordkeeping* (2nd Edition). Oakland, CA: EastHill Press, 1998.

Appendix B – References and Resources

•••*Periodicals and Publications*•••

These periodicals and publications are good sources for quick reference and potential links to additional information. Several of them have Websites that you can reference and actually get information there.

Black Enterprise   *www.blackenterprise.com*
Graves Publishing Co.
130 Fifth Avenue
New York, NY 10011

Biz Tips Newsletter   *www.bizresource.com*
Available only on-line

Business Hotline Online   *www.bizhotline.com*
Available only on-line

Colorado Business Startup Kit
Colorado Business Assistance Center
1625 Broadway, Suite 805
Denver, CO 80202

Cottage Connection
National Association for the Cottage Industry
P.O. Box 14850
Chicago, IL 60614

Entrepreneur   *www.entrepreneurmag.com*
2392 Morse Avenue
Irvine, CA 92614

Entrepreneur's Business Startups
2392 Morse Avenue
Irvine, CA 92614

Home Business Magazine   *www.homebusinessmag.com*
Research Company Inc. Box 2712
9582 Hamilton Ave, No. 368
California 92646

INC.   *www.incmag.com*
The Goldhirsch Group
P.O. Box 54129
Boulder, CO 80322

The Journal of Entrepreneurial and Small Firm Finance   *www.jaipress.com*
JAI Press, Inc.
55 Old Post Road, No. 2, Box 1678
Greenwich, CT 06830-1678

Kiplingers Personal Finance Magazine
1729 H Street, N.W.
Washington, D.C. 20006

Minority Business Entrepreneur   *www.mbemag.com*
3528 Torrance Blvd., Suite 101
Torrance, CA 90503-4803

Money Magazine   *money.com*
Time, Inc.
Time & Life Bldg., Rockefeller Center
1271 Avenue of the Americas
New York, NY 10020-1393

Small Business Tax Control   *users.aol.com/imfpubs*
Mortgage Finance Publications
Box 42387
Washington, DC 20015

Small Business Taxes & Management   *www.smbiz.com*

Smart Money   *money.com*
224 W. 57th Street
New York, NY 10019

Tax Guide for Small Business -Publication #334
Department of the Treasury
Internal Revenue Service, 1997.

Appendix B – References and Resources

•••*Accounting Software*•••

The following is a list of some of the common and most popular accounting software packages available. They are listed in alphabetical order to prevent any bias on behalf of the author.

Business Vision   *www.businessvision.com*
    7491-C5 Federal Highway, Suite 200
    Boca Raton, FL 33487
    1-800-537-4296   sales@BusinessVision.com

Business Works (20/20 Software)   *www.20-20.com/Business-Works*
    305 Mariposa Drive, Bldg. 2
    Ventura, CA 93001
    1-800-718-7348

Dac Easy Professional Accounting   *www.daceasy.com*
    SAGE US, Inc.
    17950 Preston Road, Suite 800
    Dallas, TX 75252
    (972) 818-3900

MYOB   *www.myob.com*
    300 Roundhill Drive
    Rockaway, NJ 07866
    1-800-322-MYOB(6962)

PeachTree Accounting   *www.peachtree.com*
    1505 Pavilion Place
    Norcross, GA 30093
    1-800-247-3224   sales@Peachtree.com

QuickBooks by Quicken   *www.intuit.com/quickbooks*
    P.O. Box 7850
    Mountain View, CA 94039
    1-800-224-0991

Simply Accounting   *www.simplyaccounting.com/products/simply*
    ACCPAC International
    2525 Augustine Drive
    Santa Clara, CA 95054
    (408) 562-8800

•••Websites•••

This list of Websites is by no means a comprehensive or even complete list of all the possible Websites available on recordkeeping. These are just a few sites to get you started. The list includes sites from the federal government, small business assistance groups, professional CPAs, on-line magazines and more. There are plenty other sites available for browsing, so take advantage of your search engines and get to those other locations!

1. **IRS Recommended Reading for Small Business**
   www.irs.ustreas.gov/bus_info/reading.html

2. **How to Start a Business - Recordkeeping**
   www.inreach.com/sbdc/book/recordkeeping.html
   * Prepared by San Joaquin Delta College SBDC

3. **Business Recordkeeping**
   tenonlin.org/art/bsr.html
   * A series of Ed Zimmer articles, The Entrepreneur Network

4. **The Home DayCare Complete Recordkeeping System**
   www.angelfire.com/biz/datamaster

5. **CCH Business Owner's Toolkit**
   www.toolkit.cch.com/text/P01_5100.stm

6. **CCH Small Office/Home Office Group**
   www.toolkit.cch.com

7. **Managing Your Business Finances**
   www.lowe.org/smbiznet/features/finanmgt.htm
   *Smallbiz Net featured topic series

8. **Recordkeeping in Small Business**
   www.sba.gov/sbainfo/finance-a-business/record.txt
   © 1991, Donald L. Cordano

9. **Recordkeeping in Small Business - Financial Management Series**
   www.sbaer.uca.edu/docs/publications/pub00194.txt

10. Small Business Taxes FAQ
    www.nolo.com/ChunkTAX/tax41.html

11. The Small and Home-Based Business Library
    www.bizoffice.com/library/p_r.html

12. American Express Tax FAQs
    www.americanexpress.com/smallbusiness/advice/forum/doc/taxfaqs.shtml

13. Deloitte & Touche LLP, Business Advisor
    www.dtonline.com/ba/ba.htm

14. Inc. Online
    www.inc.com

15. Legalities & Tax Advantages In a Home Business
    www.webcom.com/~seaquest/sbrc/hometax.html

•••Other Sources of Assistance•••

Most of these sources include government or government affiliated organizations. They are extremely helpful resources and often provide free training or seminars on various topics. At a minimum, you should contact them to get any information that you may find helpful. And most of the publications are free or minimal cost.

Chamber of Commerce
    Contact your city, town or state for the address of your local chamber of commerce.

Consumer Information Center (CIC)
    P.O. Box 100
    Pueblo, CO 81002

Council of Better Business Bureaus, Inc.   *www.bbb.org*
    4200 Wilson Blvd., Suite 800
    Arlington, VA 22203-1804
    Phone: (703) 276-0100
    Fax: (703) 525-8266

Federal Trade Commission   *www.ftc.gov*
    Office of Consumer Affairs
    Washington, DC 20223
    Phone: (202) 326-3284

Small Business Administration (SBA)   *www.sbaonline.sba.gov*
    1441 L Street NW
    Washington, DC 20416

Subagencies of the SBA:
    Small Business Development Centers (SBDC)
    Small Business Institutes (SBI)
    Service Corp. of Retired Executives (SCORE)

Women's Business Center (WBC)   *www.onlinewbc.org*
    *The WBC is located throughout 36 states and is affiliated with the SBA. Contact the SBA for contact information for your particular state.

APPENDIX C
Suggested IRS Publications

The following publications are ones which were chosen specifically for the sole proprietor service-oriented business. Keep in mind that you may be responsible for more than is shown here. This list is a good starting point.

Publication #225, *Farmer's Tax Guide* – identifies what types of farm income you need to report and appropriate deductions to take.

Publication #334, *Tax Guide for Small Business* – discusses federal tax laws for the sole proprietor and statutory employees.

Publication #463, *Travel, Entertainment, Gift & Car Expenses* – identifies deductible, business-related transportation, travel and entertainment expenses.

Publication #505, *Tax Withholding and Estimated Tax* – explains the two methods of paying your federal taxes.

Publication #509, *Tax Calendars for 1998* – reference this publication for information on how to use the tax calendars.

Publication #533, *Self-Employment Tax* – explains how people working for themselves determine and pay self-employment tax on their earned income (social security and medicare).

Publication #534, *Depreciating Property Place in Service Before 1987* – explains how to recover the use of business property or income-producing property by depreciation. This publication is specifcally for property placed in service **prior to** 1986.

Publication #535, *Business Expenses* – identifies common business expenses and explains what is and is not deductible.

Publication #537, *Installment Sales* – explains the tax treatment of property sales arrangement (i.e., installment sales) which provide part or all of the selling price be paid in a later year.

Publication #538, *Accounting Periods and Methods* – explains the rules for accounting periods and accounting methods.

Publication #552, *Recordkeeping for Individuals* – serves as a general reference for recordkeeping for those individuals filing an income tax.

Publication #583, *Starting a Business and Keeping Records* – provides basic federal tax information for those starting a business.

Publication #587, *Business Use of Your Home Including Use by Daycare Providers* – explains the rules for deducting your home or part of your home as a business expense.

Publication #910, *Guide to free Tax Services* – identifies the materials and services available to you from the IRS. It also indicates when and where you can get them.

Publication #917, *Business Use of Your Car* – explains how to deduct your car as a business expense and which methods to use when taking the deduction.

Publication #946, *How to Depreciate Property* – explains how to recover the use of business property or income-producing property by depreciation. This publication is specifcally for property placed in service **after** 1986.

Appendix C – Suggested IRS Publications

Publication #1518, *1998 Tax Tips Calendar for Small Businesses* – Shows all 1998 due dates for payroll deposits, paying estimated taxes and filing business tax forms.

To order free publications and forms:
By Mail: Contact your IRS Forms Distribution Center for your state

>*Eastern* Area Distribution Center
>P.O. Box 85704
>Richmond, VA 23261-5074
>
>*Central* Area Distribution Center
>P.O. Box 8903
>Bloomington, IL 61702-8903
>
>*Western* Area Distribution Center
>Rancho Cordova, CA 85743-0001

By Phone: 1-800-TAX-FORM (1-800-829-3676).

By Fax: (703) 487-4160

Local: Post office or library

Website: www.irs.ustreas.gov
Telnet: iris.irs.ustreas.gov
FTP: ftp.irs.ustreas.gov
Modem: (703) 321-8020

For additional assistance with your tax questions, access the following resources:

Tele-Tax (1-800-829-4477)
> A *free* service provided by the IRS with a prerecorded phone system designed to answer commonly asked tax questions. Tele-Tax has tax information on approximately 150 topics. It is available 24 hours a day, 7 days a week and 365 days a year.

STEP (Small Business Tax Education Program)
> With STEP, small business owners and other self-employed individuals can get more information through workshops, in-depth tax courses and instruction on starting a business, recordkeeping and various other topics. Contact the IRS directly for additional information on a locally affiliated STEP.

YBTK (Your Business Tax Kit)
> A free booklet containing IRS business tax forms and publications that can be used to prepare and file your business tax returns. Call 1-800-829-3676 to order and ask for *Your Business Tax Kit*

APPENDIX D
IRS Tax Forms

The IRS tax forms shown in this appendix represent the basic forms required for the sole proprietor. This type of legal structure generally does not require more than what is presented; however, if your business has special or extra requirements beyond what is listed here, you will need to obtain additional forms.

Form 1040A - U.S. Individual Income Tax Return

Schedule C-EZ - Net Profit From Business

Schedule C - Profit or Loss from Business (Sole Proprietorship)

Schedule SE - Self-employment Tax

Form 1040-ES - Estimated Tax

Form 4562 - Depreciation and Amortization

Form 8829 - Expenses for Business Use of Your Home

Form 1128 - Application to Adopt, Change or Retain a Tax Year

Form 3115 - Application to Change Accounting Method

104   *Organize Your Books in 6 Easy Steps*

1040A - U.S. Individual Income Tax Return (Front)

Form 1040 Department of the Treasury—Internal Revenue Service
U.S. Individual Income Tax Return (L) **1997**

For the year Jan. 1–Dec. 31, 1997, or other tax year beginning , 1997, ending , 19   OMB No. 1545-0074

IRS Use Only—Do not write or staple in this space.

Label (See instructions on page 10.)
Use the IRS label. Otherwise, please print or type.

- Your first name and initial | Last name | Your social security number
- If a joint return, spouse's first name and initial | Last name | Spouse's social security number
- Home address (number and street). If you have a P.O. box, see page 10. | Apt. no.
- City, town or post office, state, and ZIP code. If you have a foreign address, see page 10.

For help in finding line instructions, see pages 2 and 3 in the booklet.

Presidential Election Campaign (See page 10.)
- Do you want $3 to go to this fund? . . . . Yes No
- If a joint return, does your spouse want $3 to go to this fund? . . . .

Note: Checking "Yes" will not change your tax or reduce your refund.

Filing Status
Check only one box.
1. Single
2. Married filing joint return (even if only one had income)
3. Married filing separate return. Enter spouse's social security no. above and full name here. ▶ _____
4. Head of household (with qualifying person). (See page 10.) If the qualifying person is a child but not your dependent, enter this child's name here. ▶ _____
5. Qualifying widow(er) with dependent child (year spouse died ▶ 19   ). (See page 10.)

Exemptions
- 6a ☐ Yourself. If your parent (or someone else) can claim you as a dependent on his or her tax return, do not check box 6a . . . .
- b ☐ Spouse . . . .
- c Dependents:
  (1) First name Last name | (2) Dependent's social security number | (3) Dependent's relationship to you | (4) No. of months lived in your home in 1997

If more than six dependents, see page 10.

- d Total number of exemptions claimed . . . .

No. of boxes checked on 6a and 6b ___
No. of your children on 6c who:
- lived with you ___
- did not live with you due to divorce or separation (see page 11) ___
Dependents on 6c not entered above ___
Add numbers entered on lines above ▶ ___

Income

Attach Copy B of your Forms W-2, W-2G, and 1099-R here.

If you did not get a W-2, see page 12.

Enclose but do not attach any payment. Also, please use Form 1040-V.

7	Wages, salaries, tips, etc. Attach Form(s) W-2	7
8a	Taxable interest. Attach Schedule B if required	8a
b	Tax-exempt interest. DO NOT include on line 8a	8b		
9	Dividends. Attach Schedule B if required	9
10	Taxable refunds, credits, or offsets of state and local income taxes (see page 12) . .	10
11	Alimony received	11
12	Business income or (loss). Attach Schedule C or C-EZ	12
13	Capital gain or (loss). Attach Schedule D	13
14	Other gains or (losses). Attach Form 4797	14
15a	Total IRA distributions .	15a		b Taxable amount (see page 13)	15b
16a	Total pensions and annuities	16a		b Taxable amount (see page 13)	16b
17	Rental real estate, royalties, partnerships, S corporations, trusts, etc. Attach Schedule E	17
18	Farm income or (loss). Attach Schedule F	18
19	Unemployment compensation	19
20a	Social security benefits .	20a		b Taxable amount (see page 14)	20b
21	Other income. List type and amount—see page 15 _____	21
22	Add the amounts in the far right column for lines 7 through 21. This is your **total income** ▶	22

Adjusted Gross Income

If line 32 is under $29,290 (under $9,770 if a child did not live with you), see EIC inst. on page 21.

23	IRA deduction (see page 16)	23	
24	Medical savings account deduction. Attach Form 8853 .	24	
25	Moving expenses. Attach Form 3903 or 3903-F . . .	25	
26	One-half of self-employment tax. Attach Schedule SE .	26	
27	Self-employed health insurance deduction (see page 17)	27	
28	Keogh and self-employed SEP and SIMPLE plans . .	28	
29	Penalty on early withdrawal of savings	29	
30a	Alimony paid b Recipient's SSN ▶ _____	30a	
31	Add lines 23 through 30a		31
32	Subtract line 31 from line 22. This is your **adjusted gross income** . . . ▶		32

For Privacy Act and Paperwork Reduction Act Notice, see page 38.   Cat. No. 12600W   Form **1040** (1997)

Appendix D – IRS Tax Forms

1040A - U.S. Individual Income Tax Return (Back)

Form 1040 (1997) — Page 2

Tax Computation

33 Amount from line 32 (adjusted gross income) **33**

34a Check if: ☐ You were 65 or older, ☐ Blind; ☐ Spouse was 65 or older, ☐ Blind.
Add the number of boxes checked above and enter the total here . . . . . ▶ **34a**

b If you are married filing separately and your spouse itemizes deductions or you were a dual-status alien, see page 18 and check here . . . . ▶ **34b** ☐

35 Enter the larger of your:
- **Itemized deductions** from Schedule A, line 28, **OR**
- **Standard deduction** shown below for your filing status. But see page 18 if you checked any box on line 34a or 34b or someone can claim you as a dependent.
  - Single—$4,150
  - Married filing jointly or Qualifying widow(er)—$6,900
  - Head of household—$6,050
  - Married filing separately—$3,450

35

36 Subtract line 35 from line 33 . . . . **36**

If you want the IRS to figure your tax, see page 18.

37 If line 33 is $90,900 or less, multiply $2,650 by the total number of exemptions claimed on line 6d. If line 33 is over $90,900, see the worksheet on page 19 for the amount to enter . **37**

38 **Taxable income.** Subtract line 37 from line 36. If line 37 is more than line 36, enter -0- . **38**

39 Tax. See page 19. Check if any tax from **a** ☐ Form(s) 8814 **b** ☐ Form 4972 . . ▶ **39**

Credits

40 Credit for child and dependent care expenses. Attach Form 2441 . . **40**

41 Credit for the elderly or the disabled. Attach Schedule R . . . **41**

42 Adoption credit. Attach Form 8839 . . . . **42**

43 Foreign tax credit. Attach Form 1116 . . . . **43**

44 Other. Check if from **a** ☐ Form 3800 **b** ☐ Form 8396
c ☐ Form 8801 **d** ☐ Form (specify) _____ **44**

45 Add lines 40 through 44 . . . . **45**

46 Subtract line 45 from line 39. If line 45 is more than line 39, enter -0- . . . ▶ **46**

Other Taxes

47 Self-employment tax. Attach Schedule SE **47**

48 Alternative minimum tax. Attach Form 6251 . . . . **48**

49 Social security and Medicare tax on tip income not reported to employer. Attach Form 4137 . **49**

50 Tax on qualified retirement plans (including IRAs) and MSAs. Attach Form 5329 if required **50**

51 Advance earned income credit payments from Form(s) W-2 . . . . . . **51**

52 Household employment taxes. Attach Schedule H **52**

53 Add lines 46 through 52. This is your **total tax** . . . . ▶ **53**

Payments

54 Federal income tax withheld from Forms W-2 and 1099 . . **54**

55 1997 estimated tax payments and amount applied from 1996 return . **55**

56a **Earned income credit.** Attach Schedule EIC if you have a qualifying child **b** Nontaxable earned income: amount ▶ _____
and type ▶ _____ **56a**

Attach Forms W-2, W-2G, and 1099-R on the front.

57 Amount paid with Form 4868 (request for extension) . . **57**

58 Excess social security and RRTA tax withheld (see page 27) **58**

59 Other payments. Check if from **a** ☐ Form 2439 **b** ☐ Form 4136 **59**

60 Add lines 54, 55, 56a, 57, 58, and 59. These are your **total payments** . . . ▶ **60**

Refund

61 If line 60 is more than line 53, subtract line 53 from line 60. This is the amount you **OVERPAID** **61**

62a Amount of line 61 you want **REFUNDED TO YOU.** . . . . ▶ **62a**

Have it directly deposited! See page 27 and fill in 62b, 62c, and 62d.

▶ **b** Routing number [ ][ ][ ][ ][ ][ ][ ][ ][ ] ▶ **c** Type: ☐ Checking ☐ Savings

▶ **d** Account number [ ][ ][ ][ ][ ][ ][ ][ ][ ][ ][ ][ ][ ][ ][ ][ ][ ]

63 Amount of line 61 you want **APPLIED TO YOUR 1998 ESTIMATED TAX** ▶ **63**

Amount You Owe

64 If line 53 is more than line 60, subtract line 60 from line 53. This is the **AMOUNT YOU OWE.**
For details on how to pay, see page 27 . . . . ▶ **64**

65 Estimated tax penalty. Also include on line 64 . . . . . **65**

Sign Here

Under penalties of perjury, I declare that I have examined this return and accompanying schedules and statements, and to the best of my knowledge and belief, they are true, correct, and complete. Declaration of preparer (other than taxpayer) is based on all information of which preparer has any knowledge.

Keep a copy of this return for your records.

Your signature	Date	Your occupation
Spouse's signature. If a joint return, BOTH must sign.	Date	Spouse's occupation

Paid Preparer's Use Only

Preparer's signature ▶	Date	Check if self-employed ☐	Preparer's social security no.
Firm's name (or yours if self-employed) and address ▶		EIN	
		ZIP code	

Printed on recycled paper ☆ U.S. Government Printing Office: 1997 - 419 - 062

106 *Organize Your Books in 6 Easy Steps*

Schedule C-EZ - Net Profit from Business (Front)

SCHEDULE C-EZ
(Form 1040)

Department of the Treasury
Internal Revenue Service (U)

Net Profit From Business
(Sole Proprietorship)
▶ Partnerships, joint ventures, etc., must file Form 1065.
▶ Attach to Form 1040 or Form 1041. ▶ See instructions on back.

OMB No. 1545-0074

1997

Attachment Sequence No. **09A**

Name of proprietor | Social security number (SSN)

Part I — General Information

You May Use This Schedule Only If You:
- Had business expenses of $2,500 or less.
- Use the cash method of accounting.
- Did not have an inventory at any time during the year.
- Did not have a net loss from your business.
- Had only one business as a sole proprietor.

And You:
- Had no employees during the year.
- Are not required to file Form 4562, Depreciation and Amortization, for this business. See the instructions for Schedule C, line 13, on page C-3 to find out if you must file.
- Do not deduct expenses for business use of your home.
- Do not have prior year unallowed passive activity losses from this business.

A Principal business or profession, including product or service

B Enter principal business code (see page C-6) ▶

C Business name. If no separate business name, leave blank.

D Employer ID number (EIN), if any

E Business address (including suite or room no.). Address not required if same as on Form 1040, page 1.

City, town or post office, state, and ZIP code

Part II — Figure Your Net Profit

1 **Gross receipts.** Caution: *If this income was reported to you on Form W-2 and the "Statutory employee" box on that form was checked, see **Statutory Employees** in the instructions for Schedule C, line 1, on page C-2 and check here* . . . . ▶ ☐ | 1 |

2 **Total expenses.** If more than $2,500, you **must** use Schedule C. See instructions . . . . . | 2 |

3 **Net profit.** Subtract line 2 from line 1. If less than zero, you **must** use Schedule C. Enter on Form 1040, line 12, and ALSO on **Schedule SE, line 2.** (Statutory employees **do not** report this amount on Schedule SE, line 2. Estates and trusts, enter on Form 1041, line 3.) . . . . . | 3 |

Part III — Information on Your Vehicle. Complete this part ONLY if you are claiming car or truck expenses on line 2.

4 When did you place your vehicle in service for business purposes? (month, day, year) ▶ ...../...../......

5 Of the total number of miles you drove your vehicle during 1997, enter the number of miles you used your vehicle for:

a Business ....   b Commuting ....   c Other ....

6 Do you (or your spouse) have another vehicle available for personal use? . . . . ☐ Yes ☐ No

7 Was your vehicle available for use during off-duty hours? . . . . ☐ Yes ☐ No

8a Do you have evidence to support your deduction? . . . . ☐ Yes ☐ No

b If "Yes," is the evidence written? . . . . ☐ Yes ☐ No

For Paperwork Reduction Act Notice, see Form 1040 Instructions.   Cat. No. 24555U   Schedule C-EZ (Form 1040) 1997

Schedule C-EZ - Net Profit from Business (Back)

Schedule C-EZ (Form 1040) 1997 — Page 2

Instructions

You may use Schedule C-EZ instead of Schedule C if you operated a business or practiced a profession as a sole proprietorship and you have met all the requirements listed in Part I of Schedule C-EZ.

Line A
Describe the business or professional activity that provided your principal source of income reported on line 1. Give the general field or activity and the type of product or service.

Line B
Enter the four-digit code that identifies your principal business or professional activity. See page C-6 for the list of codes.

Line D
You need an employer identification number (EIN) only if you had a Keogh plan or were required to file an employment, excise, estate, trust, or alcohol, tobacco, and firearms tax return. If you need an EIN, file **Form SS-4**, Application for Employer Identification Number. If you do not have an EIN, leave line D blank. **Do not** enter your SSN.

Line E
Enter your business address. Show a street address instead of a box number. Include the suite or room number, if any.

Line 1
Enter gross receipts from your trade or business. Include amounts you received in your trade or business that were properly shown on **Forms 1099-MISC**. If the total amounts that were reported in box 7 of Forms 1099-MISC are more than the total you are reporting on line 1, attach a statement explaining the difference. You must show all items of taxable income actually or constructively received during the year (in cash, property, or services). Income is constructively received when it is credited to your account or set aside for you to use. Do not offset this amount by any losses.

Line 2
Enter the total amount of all deductible business expenses you actually paid during the year. Examples of these expenses include advertising, car and truck expenses, commissions and fees, insurance, interest, legal and professional services, office expense, rent or lease expenses, repairs and maintenance, supplies, taxes, travel, 50% of business meals and entertainment, and utilities (including telephone). For details, see the instructions for Schedule C, Parts II and V, on pages C-2 through C-5. If you wish, you may use the optional worksheet below to record your expenses.

If you claim car or truck expenses, be sure to complete Part III of Schedule C-EZ.

Optional Worksheet for Line 2 (keep a copy for your records)

a	Business meals and entertainment	a
b	Less: 50% of business meals and entertainment subject to limitations (see the instructions for lines 24b and 24c on page C-4)	b
c	Deductible business meals and entertainment. Subtract line b from line a	c
d	....	d
e	....	e
f	....	f
g	....	g
h	....	h
i	....	i
j	**Total.** Add lines c through i. Enter here and on line 2	j

Printed on recycled paper

108   *Organize Your Books in 6 Easy Steps*

Schedule C - Profit or Loss from Business (Front)

SCHEDULE C (Form 1040)
Department of the Treasury
Internal Revenue Service

Profit or Loss From Business
(Sole Proprietorship)
▶ Partnerships, joint ventures, etc., must file Form 1065.
▶ Attach to Form 1040 or Form 1041. ▶ See Instructions for Schedule C (Form 1040).

OMB No. 1545-0074
1997
Attachment Sequence No. 09

Name of proprietor | Social security number (SSN)

A Principal business or profession, including product or service (see page C-1)
B Enter principal business code (see page C-6) ▶

C Business name. If no separate business name, leave blank.
D Employer ID number (EIN), if any

E Business address (including suite or room no.) ▶ ....
     City, town or post office, state, and ZIP code

F Accounting method: (1) ☐ Cash   (2) ☐ Accrual   (3) ☐ Other (specify) ▶ ....
G Did you "materially participate" in the operation of this business during 1997? If "No," see page C-2 for limit on losses. ☐ Yes ☐ No
H If you started or acquired this business during 1997, check here . . . . ▶ ☐

Part I   Income

1. Gross receipts or sales. *Caution: If this income was reported to you on Form W-2 and the "Statutory employee" box on that form was checked, see page C-2 and check here* ▶ ☐   **1**
2. Returns and allowances **2**
3. Subtract line 2 from line 1 . . . . **3**
4. Cost of goods sold (from line 42 on page 2) **4**
5. **Gross profit.** Subtract line 4 from line 3 . . . . **5**
6. Other income, including Federal and state gasoline or fuel tax credit or refund (see page C-2) . . . **6**
7. **Gross income.** Add lines 5 and 6 . . . . ▶ **7**

Part II   Expenses. Enter expenses for business use of your home **only** on line 30.

8	Advertising	8	19	Pension and profit-sharing plans	19
9	Bad debts from sales or services (see page C-3)	9	20	Rent or lease (see page C-4):	
				a Vehicles, machinery, and equipment	20a
10	Car and truck expenses (see page C-3)	10		b Other business property	20b
			21	Repairs and maintenance	21
11	Commissions and fees	11	22	Supplies (not included in Part III)	22
12	Depletion	12	23	Taxes and licenses	23
13	Depreciation and section 179 expense deduction (not included in Part III) (see page C-3)	13	24	Travel, meals, and entertainment:	
				a Travel	24a
				b Meals and entertainment	
14	Employee benefit programs (other than on line 19)	14		c Enter 50% of line 24b subject to limitations (see page C-4)	
15	Insurance (other than health)	15			
16	Interest:			d Subtract line 24c from line 24b	24d
a	Mortgage (paid to banks, etc.)	16a	25	Utilities	25
b	Other	16b	26	Wages (less employment credits)	26
17	Legal and professional services	17	27	Other expenses (from line 48 on page 2)	27
18	Office expense	18			

28   **Total expenses** before expenses for business use of home. Add lines 8 through 27 in columns ▶ **28**

29   Tentative profit (loss). Subtract line 28 from line 7 . . . . **29**
30   Expenses for business use of your home. Attach **Form 8829** **30**
31   **Net profit or (loss).** Subtract line 30 from line 29.
     • If a profit, enter on **Form 1040, line 12,** and ALSO on **Schedule SE, line 2** (statutory employees, see page C-5). Estates and trusts, enter on **Form 1041, line 3.**   **31**
     • If a loss, you MUST go on to line 32.

32   If you have a loss, check the box that describes your investment in this activity (see page C-5).
     • If you checked 32a, enter the loss on **Form 1040, line 12,** and ALSO on **Schedule SE, line 2** (statutory employees, see page C-5). Estates and trusts, enter on **Form 1041, line 3.**
     • If you checked 32b, you MUST attach **Form 6198.**

32a ☐ All investment is at risk.
32b ☐ Some investment is not at risk.

For Paperwork Reduction Act Notice, see Form 1040 instructions.   Cat. No. 15786J   Schedule C (Form 1040) 1997

Appendix D – IRS Tax Forms

Schedule C - Profit or Loss from Business (Back)

Schedule C (Form 1040) 1997 — Page 2

Part III   Cost of Goods Sold (see page C-5)

33 Method(s) used to value closing inventory: a ☐ Cost   b ☐ Lower of cost or market   c ☐ Other (attach explanation)

34 Was there any change in determining quantities, costs, or valuations between opening and closing inventory? If "Yes," attach explanation . . . . ☐ Yes ☐ No

35 Inventory at beginning of year. If different from last year's closing inventory, attach explanation . . | 35 |

36 Purchases less cost of items withdrawn for personal use . . . . | 36 |

37 Cost of labor. Do not include salary paid to yourself . . . . | 37 |

38 Materials and supplies . . . . | 38 |

39 Other costs . . . . | 39 |

40 Add lines 35 through 39 . . . . | 40 |

41 Inventory at end of year . . . . | 41 |

42 **Cost of goods sold.** Subtract line 41 from line 40. Enter the result here and on page 1, line 4 . . | 42 |

Part IV   Information on Your Vehicle. Complete this part ONLY if you are claiming car or truck expenses on line 10 and are not required to file Form 4562 for this business. See the instructions for line 13 on page C-3 to find out if you must file.

43 When did you place your vehicle in service for business purposes? (month, day, year) ▶ ...... / ...... / ....

44 Of the total number of miles you drove your vehicle during 1997, enter the number of miles you used your vehicle for:

   a Business .... b Commuting .... c Other ....

45 Do you (or your spouse) have another vehicle available for personal use? . . . . ☐ Yes ☐ No

46 Was your vehicle available for use during off-duty hours? . . . . ☐ Yes ☐ No

47a Do you have evidence to support your deduction? . . . . ☐ Yes ☐ No

   b If "Yes," is the evidence written? . . . . ☐ Yes ☐ No

Part V   Other Expenses. List below business expenses not included on lines 8–26 or line 30.

48 Total other expenses. Enter here and on page 1, line 27 . . . . | 48 |

Printed on recycled paper

110   *Organize Your Books in 6 Easy Steps*

Schedule SE - Self-employment Tax (Front)

SCHEDULE SE (Form 1040)
Department of the Treasury
Internal Revenue Service (O)

Self-Employment Tax

▶ See Instructions for Schedule SE (Form 1040).

▶ Attach to Form 1040.

OMB No. 1545-0074

1997

Attachment Sequence No. **17**

Name of person with **self-employment** income (as shown on Form 1040) | Social security number of person with **self-employment** income ▶

Who Must File Schedule SE
You must file Schedule SE if:
- You had net earnings from self-employment from **other than** church employee income (line 4 of Short Schedule SE or line 4c of Long Schedule SE) of $400 or more, **OR**
- You had church employee income of $108.28 or more. Income from services you performed as a minister or a member of a religious order **is not** church employee income. See page SE-1.

Note: *Even if you had a loss or a small amount of income from self-employment, it may be to your benefit to file Schedule SE and use either "optional method" in Part II of Long Schedule SE. See page SE-3.*

Exception. If your only self-employment income was from earnings as a minister, member of a religious order, or Christian Science practitioner **and** you filed Form 4361 and received IRS approval not to be taxed on those earnings, **do not** file Schedule SE. Instead, write "Exempt–Form 4361" on Form 1040, line 47.

May I Use Short Schedule SE or MUST I Use Long Schedule SE?

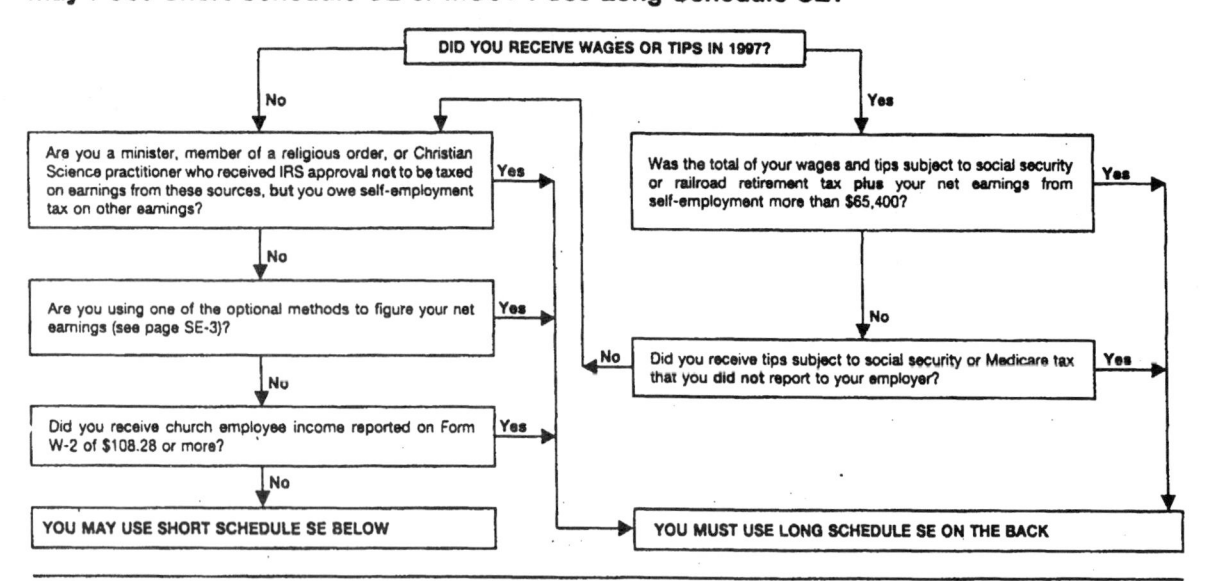

```
                    DID YOU RECEIVE WAGES OR TIPS IN 1997?
                    /                                    \
                  No                                    Yes
                   │                                     │
   ┌───────────────────────────────┐      ┌──────────────────────────────────┐
   │ Are you a minister, member of │      │ Was the total of your wages and  │
   │ a religious order, or Christian│ Yes │ tips subject to social security  │ Yes
   │ Science practitioner who      │─────▶│ or railroad retirement tax plus  │────▶
   │ received IRS approval not to  │      │ your net earnings from           │
   │ be taxed on earnings from     │      │ self-employment more than        │
   │ these sources, but you owe    │      │ $65,400?                         │
   │ self-employment tax on other  │      └──────────────────────────────────┘
   │ earnings?                     │                      │
   └───────────────────────────────┘                     No
                 │                                        │
                No                                        ▼
                 ▼                          ┌──────────────────────────────────┐
   ┌───────────────────────────────┐        │ Did you receive tips subject to  │
   │ Are you using one of the      │  Yes   │ social security or Medicare tax  │ Yes
   │ optional methods to figure    │───No──▶│ that you did not report to your  │────▶
   │ your net earnings (see page   │        │ employer?                        │
   │ SE-3)?                        │        └──────────────────────────────────┘
   └───────────────────────────────┘
                 │
                No
                 ▼
   ┌───────────────────────────────┐
   │ Did you receive church        │ Yes
   │ employee income reported on   │────▶
   │ Form W-2 of $108.28 or more?  │
   └───────────────────────────────┘
                 │
                No
                 ▼
   YOU MAY USE SHORT SCHEDULE SE BELOW       YOU MUST USE LONG SCHEDULE SE ON THE BACK
```

Section A—Short Schedule SE. Caution: *Read above to see if you can use Short Schedule SE.*

1	Net farm profit or (loss) from Schedule F, line 36, and farm partnerships, Schedule K-1 (Form 1065), line 15a	**1**
2	Net profit or (loss) from Schedule C, line 31; Schedule C-EZ, line 3; and Schedule K-1 (Form 1065), line 15a (other than farming). Ministers and members of religious orders, see page SE-1 for amounts to report on this line. See page SE-2 for other income to report	**2**
3	Combine lines 1 and 2	**3**
4	**Net earnings from self-employment.** Multiply line 3 by 92.35% (.9235). If less than $400, do not file this schedule; you do not owe self-employment tax . . . . ▶	**4**
5	**Self-employment tax.** If the amount on line 4 is: • $65,400 or less, multiply line 4 by 15.3% (.153). Enter the result here and on **Form 1040, line 47.** • More than $65,400, multiply line 4 by 2.9% (.029). Then, add $8,109.60 to the result. Enter the total here and on **Form 1040, line 47.**	**5**
6	**Deduction for one-half of self-employment tax.** Multiply line 5 by 50% (.5). Enter the result here and on **Form 1040, line 26**	**6**	

For Paperwork Reduction Act Notice, see Form 1040 instructions.   Cat. No. 11358Z   Schedule SE (Form 1040) 1997

Schedule SE - Self-employment Tax (Back)

Schedule SE (Form 1040) 1997 — Attachment Sequence No. 17 — Page 2

Name of person with **self-employment** income (as shown on Form 1040) | Social security number of person with **self-employment** income ▶

Section B—Long Schedule SE

Part I Self-Employment Tax

Note: *If your only income subject to self-employment tax is* **church employee income**, *skip lines 1 through 4b. Enter -0- on line 4c and go to line 5a. Income from services you performed as a minister or a member of a religious order is* **not** *church employee income. See page SE-1.*

A If you are a minister, member of a religious order, or Christian Science practitioner **and** you filed Form 4361, but you had $400 or more of **other** net earnings from self-employment, check here and continue with Part I . . . . ▶ ☐

1	Net farm profit or (loss) from Schedule F, line 36, and farm partnerships, Schedule K-1 (Form 1065), line 15a. **Note:** *Skip this line if you use the farm optional method. See page SE-3*	1
2	Net profit or (loss) from Schedule C, line 31; Schedule C-EZ, line 3; and Schedule K-1 (Form 1065), line 15a (other than farming). Ministers and members of religious orders, see page SE-1 for amounts to report on this line. See page SE-2 for other income to report. **Note:** *Skip this line if you use the nonfarm optional method. See page SE-3.*	2
3	Combine lines 1 and 2	3
4a	If line 3 is more than zero, multiply line 3 by 92.35% (.9235). Otherwise, enter amount from line 3	4a
b	If you elected one or both of the optional methods, enter the total of lines 15 and 17 here	4b
c	Combine lines 4a and 4b. If less than $400, **do not** file this schedule; you do not owe self-employment tax. **Exception.** If less than $400 and you had **church employee income**, enter -0- and continue ▶	4c
5a	Enter your **church employee income** from Form W-2. **Caution:** *See page SE-1 for definition of church employee income* . . . 5a	
b	Multiply line 5a by 92.35% (.9235). If less than $100, enter -0-	5b
6	**Net earnings from self-employment.** Add lines 4c and 5b	6
7	Maximum amount of combined wages and self-employment earnings subject to social security tax or the 6.2% portion of the 7.65% railroad retirement (tier 1) tax for 1997	7	65,400	00
8a	Total social security wages and tips (total of boxes 3 and 7 on Form(s) W-2) and railroad retirement (tier 1) compensation . . . 8a	
b	Unreported tips subject to social security tax (from Form 4137, line 9) 8b	
c	Add lines 8a and 8b	8c
9	Subtract line 8c from line 7. If zero or less, enter -0- here and on line 10 and go to line 11 ▶	9
10	Multiply the **smaller** of line 6 or line 9 by 12.4% (.124)	10
11	Multiply line 6 by 2.9% (.029)	11
12	**Self-employment tax.** Add lines 10 and 11. Enter here and on **Form 1040, line 47**	12
13	**Deduction for one-half of self-employment tax.** Multiply line 12 by 50% (.5). Enter the result here and on **Form 1040, line 26** . . . 13	

Part II Optional Methods To Figure Net Earnings (See page SE-3.)

Farm Optional Method. You may use this method **only** if:
- Your gross farm income[1] was not more than $2,400, **or**
- Your gross farm income[1] was more than $2,400 and your net farm profits[2] were less than $1,733.

14	Maximum income for optional methods	14	1,600	00
15	Enter the **smaller** of: two-thirds (⅔) of gross farm income[1] (not less than zero) or $1,600. Also, include this amount on line 4b above	15		

Nonfarm Optional Method. You may use this method **only** if:
- Your net nonfarm profits[3] were less than $1,733 and also less than 72.189% of your gross nonfarm income,[4] **and**
- You had net earnings from self-employment of at least $400 in 2 of the prior 3 years.

Caution: *You may use this method no more than five times.*

16	Subtract line 15 from line 14	16	
17	Enter the **smaller** of: two-thirds (⅔) of gross nonfarm income[4] (not less than zero) or the amount on line 16. Also, include this amount on line 4b above	17	

[1] From Schedule F, line 11, and Schedule K-1 (Form 1065), line 15b.
[2] From Schedule F, line 36, and Schedule K-1 (Form 1065), line 15a.
[3] From Schedule C, line 31; Schedule C-EZ, line 3; and Schedule K-1 (Form 1065), line 15a.
[4] From Schedule C, line 7; Schedule C-EZ, line 1; and Schedule K-1 (Form 1065), line 15c.

Appendix D – IRS Tax Forms

112 *Organize Your Books in 6 Easy Steps*

Form 1040-ES - Estimated Tax (Page 1)

Form **1040-ES**	**Estimated Tax for Individuals**	OMB No. 1545-0087
Department of the Treasury Internal Revenue Service	This package is primarily for first-time filers of estimated tax.	1998

Purpose of This Package

Use this package to figure and pay your estimated tax. Estimated tax is the method used to pay tax on income that is not subject to withholding (for example, earnings from self-employment, interest, dividends, rents, alimony, etc.). In addition, if you do not elect voluntary withholding, you should make estimated tax payments on unemployment compensation and the taxable part of your social security benefits. See the 1997 instructions for your tax return for more details on income that is taxable.

This package is primarily for first-time filers who are or may be subject to paying estimated tax. This package can also be used if you did not receive or have lost your preprinted 1040-ES package. The estimated tax worksheet on page 4 will help you figure the correct amount to pay. The payment vouchers in this package are for crediting your estimated tax payments to your account correctly. Use the **Record of Estimated Tax Payments** on page 6 to keep track of the payments you have made and the number and amount of your remaining payments.

After we receive your first payment voucher from this package, we will mail you a 1040-ES package with your name, address, and social security number preprinted on each payment voucher. Use the preprinted vouchers to make your **remaining** estimated tax payments for the year. This will speed processing, reduce processing costs, and reduce the chance of errors.

Do not use the vouchers in this package to notify the IRS of a **change of address.** If you have a new address, complete **Form 8822,** Change of Address, and send it to the Internal Revenue Service Center at the address shown in the Form 8822 instructions. The service center will update your record and send you new preprinted payment vouchers.

Note: *Continue to use your old preprinted payment vouchers to make payments of estimated tax until you receive the new vouchers.*

Who Must Make Estimated Tax Payments

In most cases, you must make estimated tax payments if you expect to owe at least $1,000 in tax for 1998 (after subtracting your withholding and credits) and you expect your withholding and credits to be less than the **smaller** of:

1. 90% of the tax shown on your 1998 tax return, **or**
2. The tax shown on your 1997 tax return.

However, if you did not file a 1997 tax return or that return did not cover all 12 months, item 2 above does not apply.

For this purpose, include household employment taxes when figuring the tax shown on your tax return, but **only** if **either** of the following is true:

- You will have Federal income tax withheld from wages, pensions, annuities, gambling winnings, or other income, **or**
- You would be required to make estimated tax payments to avoid a penalty even if you did not include household employment taxes when figuring your estimated tax.

Exception. You do not have to pay estimated tax if you were a U.S. citizen or resident alien for all of 1997 and you had no tax liability for the full 12-month 1997 tax year.

The estimated tax rules apply to:

- U.S. citizens and residents,
- Residents of Puerto Rico, the Virgin Islands, Guam, the Commonwealth of the Northern Mariana Islands, and American Samoa, and
- Nonresident aliens (use Form 1040-ES (NR)).

If you also receive salaries and wages, you may be able to avoid having to make estimated tax payments on your other income by asking your employer to take more tax out of your earnings. To do this, file a new **Form W-4,** Employee's Withholding Allowance Certificate, with your employer.

You can also choose to have Federal income tax withheld on certain government payments. For details, see **Form W-4V,** Voluntary Withholding Request.

Caution: *You may not make joint estimated tax payments if you or your spouse is a nonresident alien, you are separated under a decree of divorce or separate maintenance, or you and your spouse have different tax years.*

Additional Information You May Need

Most of the information you will need can be found in:
Pub. 505, Tax Withholding and Estimated Tax.
Other available information:

- **Pub. 553,** Highlights of 1997 Tax Changes.
- Instructions for the 1997 Form 1040 or 1040A.
- **What's Hot** at www.irs.ustreas.gov.

For details on how to get forms and publications, see page 4 of the instructions for Form 1040 or 1040A.

If you have tax questions, call 1-800-829-1040 for assistance.

Tax Law Changes Effective for 1998

Use your 1997 tax return as a guide in figuring your 1998 estimated tax, but be sure to consider the changes noted in this section. For more information on changes that may affect your 1998 estimated tax, see Pub. 553.

Estimated tax payments of household employment taxes. Beginning in 1998, you must **include** household employment taxes when figuring your estimated tax payments if **either** of the following applies for the year:

- You will have Federal income tax withheld from wages, pensions, annuities, gambling winnings, or other income, **or**
- You would be required to make estimated tax payments (to avoid a penalty) even if you **did not** include household employment taxes when figuring your estimated tax.

Increase in amount of tax exempt from estimated tax requirements. Beginning in 1998, the requirement to make estimated tax payments (to avoid a penalty) will not apply unless the tax you owe, after subtracting withholding and other credits, is at least $1,000.

Modification of estimated tax safe harbor for some taxpayers. For 1998, the estimated tax safe harbor that is based on the tax shown on the prior year tax return is the same for all taxpayers (except for farmers and fishermen), regardless of adjusted gross income (AGI). That safe harbor is 100% of the tax shown on the 1997 tax return.

Child tax credit. For 1998, you may be entitled to a $400 credit for each of your dependent children who is under age 17 on December 31, 1998. The credit is subject to limits based on your tax, and a phaseout, which begins when your modified AGI exceeds $75,000 ($110,000 if married filing jointly or qualifying widow(er); $55,000 if married filing separately). Above this level, the credit is reduced by $50 for each $1,000 (or fraction thereof) of modified AGI.

Credits for higher education expenses. You may be able to claim the *Hope Scholarship Credit* for tuition and related expenses you pay in 1998 for yourself, your spouse, or dependents to enroll at or attend an eligible educational institution. This credit applies only to the first 2 years of postsecondary education. The student must be enrolled in a degree, certificate, or other program leading to a recognized

Cat. No. 11340T *(Continued on page 2)*

Form 1040-ES - Estimated Tax (Page 2)

credential at an eligible educational institution and must carry at least one-half of a normal full-time work load. The maximum credit per student is $1,500 (100% of the first $1,000 of qualified tuition and related expenses, plus 50% of the next $1,000 of such expenses).

For qualified expenses paid after June 30, 1998, you may be able to claim the *Lifetime Learning Credit*. This credit does not require enrollment in a degree or other program and may be claimed for undergraduate, graduate, or professional degree expenses or for any course at an accredited institution of higher education that helps the student acquire or improve job skills. The credit is 20% of up to $5,000 of qualified tuition and related expenses (the maximum credit per tax return is $1,000).

These credits are available only for expenses paid during the tax year for an academic period beginning in that tax year and cannot be claimed for the cost of books, room and board, or similar expenses. You **cannot** claim either credit if you are married filing separately or you are claimed as a dependent on another person's 1998 tax return.

Each credit is subject to a limit based on your tax and is phased out ratably over a range that:
- Begins when your modified AGI exceeds $40,000 ($80,000 if married filing jointly or qualifying widow(er)), and
- Ends at $50,000 ($100,000 if married filing jointly or qualifying widow(er)).

Caution: *You may not claim both the Hope Scholarship Credit and the Lifetime Learning Credit on behalf of the same student in 1998. Also, you may not claim either of these credits for expenses incurred on behalf of a student in any year in which you also exclude distributions from an education IRA to pay higher education costs for that student.*

Student loan interest. You may be allowed to deduct up to $1,000 for interest due after 1997 that is paid during 1998 on a qualified higher education loan you used to pay for education expenses for yourself, your spouse, or a dependent. A loan made by a related person is not a qualified loan. The deduction is allowed in arriving at AGI (i.e., you do not have to itemize deductions to claim it). The student must have been enrolled in a degree, certificate, or other program leading to a recognized credential at an eligible educational institution and must have carried at least one-half of a normal full-time work load. The deduction is allowed only during the first 60 months in which interest payments are required.

The deduction is phased out ratably over a range that:
- Begins when your modified AGI exceeds $40,000 ($60,000 if married filing jointly or qualifying widow(er)), and
- Ends at $55,000 ($75,000 if married filing jointly or qualifying widow(er)).

You **cannot** take this deduction if you are claimed as a dependent on another person's 1998 tax return or you are married filing a separate return.

IRA deduction increased or restored for some people covered by retirement plans. The income limits for claiming an IRA deduction for 1998 have been increased if you are covered by a retirement plan. Under the new rules, the deduction is phased out ratably over a range that:
- Begins when your modified AGI exceeds $30,000 ($50,000 if married filing jointly or qualifying widow(er)), and
- Ends at $40,000 ($60,000 if married filing jointly or qualifying widow(er)).

Also, if your spouse is covered by a retirement plan but you are not, you are eligible beginning in 1998 to claim an IRA deduction (unless you are married filing a separate return). In this case, the maximum IRA deduction is phased out ratably over a range that begins at a modified AGI of $150,000 and ends at $160,000.

Distributions from IRAs to pay for qualified higher education expenses or "first-time homebuyer" expenses. Beginning with distributions made after 1997, the 10% tax on an early distribution from an IRA will not apply if you use the distribution to pay for either of the following:
- Qualified higher education expenses for academic periods beginning after 1997 for yourself, your spouse, child, grandchild, stepchild, or step-grandchild for attendance at an accredited institution of higher education.
- Certain expenses incurred to buy, build, or rebuild a "first" home that is your main home, your spouse's main home, or the main home of a child, grandchild, or ancestor of yours or your spouse's. Distributions used for this purpose are subject to a lifetime limit of $10,000. In most cases, a home is considered your "first" home if you had no present ownership in a main home during the 2-year period ending on the date you acquired your new home.

(Continued on page 3)

1998 Tax Rate Schedules

Caution: *Do not use these Tax Rate Schedules to figure your 1997 taxes. Use only to figure your 1998 estimated taxes.*

Single—Schedule X

If line 5 is: Over—	But not over—	The tax is:	of the amount over—
$0	$25,350	.........15%	$0
25,350	61,400	$3,802.50 + 28%	25,350
61,400	128,100	13,896.50 + 31%	61,400
128,100	278,450	34,573.50 + 36%	128,100
278,450	....	88,699.50 + 39.6%	278,450

Head of household—Schedule Z

If line 5 is: Over—	But not over—	The tax is:	of the amount over—
$0	$33,950	.........15%	$0
33,950	87,700	$5,092.50 + 28%	33,950
87,700	142,000	20,142.50 + 31%	87,700
142,000	278,450	36,975.50 + 36%	142,000
278,450	....	86,097.50 + 39.6%	278,450

Married filing jointly or Qualifying widow(er)—Schedule Y-1

If line 5 is: Over—	But not over—	The tax is:	of the amount over—
$0	$42,350	.........15%	$0
42,350	102,300	$6,352.50 + 28%	42,350
102,300	155,950	23,138.50 + 31%	102,300
155,950	278,450	39,770.00 + 36%	155,950
278,450	....	83,870.00 + 39.6%	278,450

Married filing separately—Schedule Y-2

If line 5 is: Over—	But not over—	The tax is:	of the amount over—
$0	$21,175	.........15%	$0
21,175	51,150	$3,176.25 + 28%	21,175
51,150	77,975	11,569.25 + 31%	51,150
77,975	139,225	19,885.00 + 36%	77,975
139,225	....	41,935.00 + 39.6%	139,225

Page 2

Form 1040-ES - Estimated Tax (Page 3)

Foreign earned income exclusion. For 1998, the maximum foreign earned income exclusion amount has been increased to $72,000.

Section 179 expense deduction increased. For 1998, the deduction to expense certain property under section 179 generally has been increased to $18,500.

Self-employed health insurance deduction increased. For 1998, the self-employed health insurance deduction is increased to 45% of health insurance expenses.

Matching contributions to 401(k) plans of self-employed individuals. Generally, matching contributions made for tax years after 1997 to 401(k) plans of self-employed persons are not treated as elective employer contributions and therefore are not subject to the $10,000 annual limit on elective contributions.

Welfare-to-work credit. Employers that pay wages to long-term family assistance recipients may qualify for the welfare-to-work credit. This new credit is based on wages paid to qualified individuals who begin work after December 31, 1997. For more details, see **Form 8861**, Welfare-to-Work Credit.

Income averaging for farmers. Starting in 1998, farmers may elect to average farm income over the 3 prior tax years. This election does not affect the computation of self-employment tax.

Standard deduction for 1998. If you do not itemize your deductions, you may take the 1998 standard deduction listed below:

Filing Status	Standard Deduction
Married filing jointly or Qualifying widow(er)	$7,100
Head of household	$6,250
Single	$4,250
Married filing separately	$3,550

However, if you can be claimed as a dependent on another person's 1998 return, your standard deduction is the greater of:
- $700, or
- Your earned income plus $250 (up to the standard deduction amount).

An additional amount is added to the standard deduction if:

1. You are an unmarried individual (single or head of household) and are:

65 or older or blind	$1,050
65 or older and blind	$2,100

2. You are a married individual (filing jointly or separately) or a qualifying widow(er) and are:

65 or older or blind	$850
65 or older and blind	$1,700
Both spouses 65 or older	$1,700*
Both spouses 65 or older and blind	$3,400*

* If married filing separately, these amounts apply only if you can claim an exemption for your spouse.

To Figure Your Estimated Tax Use:

- The **1998 Estimated Tax Worksheet** on page 4.
- The instructions on this page for the worksheet on page 4.
- The **1998 Tax Rate Schedules** on page 2.
- Your 1997 tax return and instructions as a guide to figuring your income, deductions, and credits (but be sure to consider the tax law changes noted earlier).

If you receive your income unevenly throughout the year (e.g., you operate your business on a seasonal basis), you may be able to lower or eliminate the amount of your required estimated tax payment for one or more periods by using the annualized income installment method. See Pub. 505 for details.

To amend or correct your estimated tax, see **Amending Estimated Tax Payments** on page 4.

Instructions for Worksheet on Page 4

Line 1—Use your 1997 tax return and instructions as a guide to figuring the adjusted gross income you expect in 1998 (but be sure to consider the tax law changes noted earlier). For more details on figuring your adjusted gross income, see **Expected Adjusted Gross Income** in Pub. 505. If you are self-employed, be sure to take into account the deduction for one-half of your self-employment tax.

Line 7—Additional Taxes. Enter the additional taxes from **Form 4972**, Tax on Lump-Sum Distributions, or **Form 8814**, Parents' Election To Report Child's Interest and Dividends.

Line 9—Credits. See the 1997 Form 1040, lines 40 through 45, or Form 1040A, lines 24a, 24b, and 24c, and the related instructions.

Line 11—Self-Employment Tax. If you and your spouse make joint estimated tax payments and you both have self-employment income, figure the self-employment tax for each of you separately. Enter the total on line 11. When figuring your estimate of 1998 net earnings from self-employment, be sure to use only 92.35% of your total net profit from self-employment.

Line 12—Other Taxes. Except as noted below, enter any other taxes, such as alternative minimum tax, tax on accumulation distribution of trusts, tax on a distribution from an MSA, and the tax on early distributions from **(a)** a qualified retirement plan (including your IRA), **(b)** an annuity, or **(c)** a modified endowment contract entered into after June 20, 1988.

Include household employment taxes on line 12 if **either** of the following is true:
- You will have Federal income tax withheld from wages, pensions, annuities, gambling winnings, or other income, **or**
- You would be required to make estimated tax payments (to avoid a penalty) even if you did not include household employment taxes when figuring your estimated tax.

Do not include tax on recapture of a Federal mortgage subsidy, social security and Medicare tax on unreported tip income, or uncollected employee social security and Medicare or RRTA tax on tips or group-term life insurance. These taxes are not required to be paid until your income tax return is due (not including extensions).

Payment Due Dates

You may pay all of your estimated tax by April 15, 1998, or in four equal amounts by the dates shown below:

1st payment	April 15, 1998
2nd payment	June 15, 1998
3rd payment	Sept. 15, 1998
4th payment	Jan. 15, 1999*

*You do not have to make the payment due January 15, 1999, if you file your 1998 tax return by February 1, 1999, **AND** pay the entire balance due with your return.

Note: Payments are due by the dates indicated whether or not you are outside the United States and Puerto Rico.

If, after March 31, 1998, you have a large change in income, deductions, additional taxes, or credits that requires you to start making estimated tax payments, you should figure the amount of your estimated tax payments by using the annualized income installment method, as explained in Pub. 505. Although your payment due dates will be the same as shown above, the payment amounts will vary based on your income, deductions, additional taxes, and credits for the months ending before each payment due date. As a result, this method may allow you to skip or lower the amount due for one or more payments. If you use the annualized income installment method, be sure to file **Form 2210**, Underpayment of Estimated Tax by Individuals, Estates, and Trusts, with your 1998 tax return, even if no penalty is owed.

(Continued on page 4)

Form 1040-ES - Estimated Tax (Page 4)

Farmers and fishermen. If at least two-thirds of your gross income for 1997 or 1998 is from farming or fishing, you may do one of the following:
- Pay all of your estimated tax by January 15, 1999, or
- File your 1998 Form 1040 by March 1, 1999, and pay the total tax due. In this case, 1998 estimated payments are not required.

Fiscal year taxpayers. You are on a fiscal year if your 12-month tax period ends on any day except December 31. Due dates for fiscal year taxpayers are the 15th day of the 4th, 6th, and 9th months of your current fiscal year and the 1st month of the following fiscal year. If any payment date falls on a Saturday, Sunday, or legal holiday, use the next business day.

Amending Estimated Tax Payments

To change or amend your estimated payments, refigure your total estimated payments due (line 16 of the worksheet below). Then use the worksheets under **Amended estimated tax** in Chapter 2 of Pub. 505 to figure the payment due for each remaining payment period. If an estimated tax payment for a previous period is less than one-fourth of your amended estimated tax, you may owe a penalty when you file your return.

(Continued on page 5)

1998 Estimated Tax Worksheet (keep for your records)

1	Enter amount of adjusted gross income you expect in 1998 (see instructions)	1
2	• If you plan to itemize deductions, enter the estimated total of your itemized deductions. **Caution:** If line 1 above is over $124,500 ($62,250 if married filing separately), your deduction may be reduced. See Pub. 505 for details. • If you do not plan to itemize deductions, see **Standard Deduction for 1998** on page 3, and enter your standard deduction here.	2
3	Subtract line 2 from line 1	3
4	Exemptions. Multiply $2,700 by the number of personal exemptions. If you can be claimed as a dependent on another person's 1998 return, your personal exemption is not allowed. **Caution:** If line 1 above is over $186,800 ($155,650 if head of household; $124,500 if single; $93,400 if married filing separately), see Pub. 505 to figure the amount to enter	4
5	Subtract line 4 from line 3	5
6	**Tax.** Figure your tax on the amount on line 5 by using the 1998 Tax Rate Schedules on page 2. DO NOT use the Tax Table or the Tax Rate Schedules in the 1997 Form 1040 or Form 1040A instructions. **Caution:** If you have a net capital gain, see Pub. 505 to figure the tax.	6
7	Additional taxes (see instructions)	7
8	Add lines 6 and 7	8
9	Credits (see instructions). Do not include any income tax withholding on this line	9
10	Subtract line 9 from line 8. Enter the result, but not less than zero	10
11	Self-employment tax (see instructions). Estimate of 1998 net earnings from self-employment $.............. ; if **$68,400 or less,** multiply the amount by 15.3%; if **more than $68,400,** multiply the amount by 2.9%, add $8,481.60 to the result, and enter the total. **Caution:** If you also have wages subject to social security tax, see Pub. 505 to figure the amount to enter	11
12	Other taxes (see instructions)	12
13a	Add lines 10 through 12	13a
b	Earned income credit and credit from **Form 4136**	13b
c	Subtract line 13b from line 13a. Enter the result, but not less than zero. **THIS IS YOUR TOTAL 1998 ESTIMATED TAX** ▶	13c
14a	Multiply line 13c by 90% (66⅔% for farmers and fishermen) . . . 14a	
b	Enter the tax shown on your 1997 tax return 14b	
c	Enter the **smaller** of line 14a or 14b. **THIS IS YOUR REQUIRED ANNUAL PAYMENT TO AVOID A PENALTY** ▶	14c
	Caution: Generally, if you do not prepay (through income tax withholding and estimated tax payments) at least the amount on line 14c, you may owe a penalty for not paying enough estimated tax. To avoid a penalty, make sure your estimate on line 13c is as accurate as possible. Even if you pay the required annual payment, you may still owe tax when you file your return. If you prefer, you may pay the amount shown on line 13c. For more details, see Pub. 505.	
15	Income tax withheld and estimated to be withheld during 1998 (including income tax withholding on pensions, annuities, certain deferred income, etc.)	15
16	Subtract line 15 from line 14c. (**Note:** If zero or less, or line 13c minus line 15 is less than $1,000, stop here. You are not required to make estimated tax payments.)	16
17	If the first payment you are required to make is due April 15, 1998, enter ¼ of line 16 (minus any 1997 overpayment that you are applying to this installment) here and on your payment voucher(s)	17

Form 1040-ES - Estimated Tax (Page 5)

When a Penalty Is Applied

In some cases, you may owe a penalty when you file your return. The penalty is imposed on each underpayment for the number of days it remains unpaid. A penalty may be applied if you did not pay enough estimated tax for the year, or you did not make the payments on time or in the required amount. A penalty may apply even if you have an overpayment on your tax return.

The penalty may be waived under certain conditions. See Pub. 505 for details.

How To Complete and Use the Payment Voucher

There is a separate payment voucher for each due date. The due date is shown in the upper right corner. Please be sure you use the voucher with the correct due date for each payment you make. Complete and send in the voucher **only** if you are making a payment. To complete your voucher:

- Type or print your name, address, and social security number in the space provided on the voucher. If filing a joint voucher, also enter your spouse's name and social security number. List the names and social security numbers in the same order on the joint voucher as you will on your joint return. If you and your spouse plan to file separate returns, file separate vouchers instead of a joint voucher.
- Enter on the payment line of the voucher only the amount you are sending in. When making payments of estimated tax, be sure to take into account any 1997 overpayment that you choose to credit against your 1998 tax, but do not include the overpayment amount on this line.
- Enclose your payment, making the check or money order payable to: "Internal Revenue Service" (not "IRS").
- Write your social security number and "1998 Form 1040-ES" on your check or money order.
- Do not staple or attach your payment to the voucher.
- Mail your payment voucher to the address shown on page 6 for the place where you live.
- Fill in the **Record of Estimated Tax Payments** on page 6 for your files.

If you changed your name and made estimated tax payments using your old name, attach a statement to the front of your 1998 tax return. List all of the estimated tax payments you and your spouse made for 1998, the address where you made the payments, and the name(s) and social security number(s) under which you made the payments.

Paperwork Reduction Act Notice. We ask for the information on the payment vouchers to carry out the Internal Revenue laws of the United States. You are required to give us the information. We need it to ensure that you are complying with these laws and to allow us to figure and collect the right amount of tax.

You are not required to provide the information requested on a form that is subject to the Paperwork Reduction Act unless the form displays a valid OMB control number. Books or records relating to a form or its instructions must be retained as long as their contents may become material in the administration of any Internal Revenue law. Generally, tax returns and return information are confidential, as required by Internal Revenue Code section 6103.

The time needed to complete the worksheets and prepare and file the payment vouchers will vary depending on individual circumstances. The estimated average time is: **Recordkeeping,** 1 hr., 19 min.; **Learning about the law,** 22 min.; **Preparing the worksheets and payment vouchers,** 49 min.; **Copying, assembling, and sending the payment voucher to the IRS,** 10 min. If you have comments concerning the accuracy of these time estimates or suggestions for making this package simpler, we would be happy to hear from you. You can write to the Tax Forms Committee, Western Area Distribution Center, Rancho Cordova, CA 95743-0001. **DO NOT** send the payment vouchers to this address. Instead, see **Where To File Your Payment Voucher** on page 6.

Tear off here

Form 1040-ES
Department of the Treasury
Internal Revenue Service

1998 Payment Voucher 4

OMB No. 1545-0087

File only if you are making a payment of estimated tax. Return this voucher with check or money order payable to the **"Internal Revenue Service."** Please write your social security number and "1998 Form 1040-ES" on your check or money order. Do not send cash. Enclose, but do not staple or attach, your payment with this voucher.

Calendar year—Due Jan. 15, 1999

Amount of payment	Please type or print	Your first name and initial	Your last name	Your social security number
$		If joint payment, complete for spouse		
		Spouse's first name and initial	Spouse's last name	Spouse's social security number
		Address (number, street, and apt. no.)		
		City, state, and ZIP code (If a foreign address, enter city, province or state, postal code, and country.)		

For Paperwork Reduction Act Notice, see instructions on page 5.

Page 5

Appendix D – IRS Tax Forms

Form 1040-ES - Estimated Tax (Page 6)

Record of Estimated Tax Payments (see page 3 for payment due dates)

Payment number	(a) Date	(b) Check or money order number	(c) Amount paid	(d) 1997 overpayment credit applied	(e) Total amount paid and credited (add (c) and (d))
1					
2					
3					
4					
Total ▶					

Where To File Your Payment Voucher

Mail your payment voucher to the Internal Revenue Service at the address shown below for the place where you live. **Do not** mail your tax return to this address. Also, do not mail your estimated tax payments to the address shown in the Form 1040 or 1040A instructions.

Note: *For proper delivery of your estimated tax payment to a P.O. box, you must include the box number in the address. Also, note that only the U.S. Postal Service can deliver to P.O. boxes.*

If you live in:	Use this address:
New Jersey, New York (New York City and counties of Nassau, Rockland, Suffolk, and Westchester)	P.O. Box 162 Newark, NJ 07101-0162
New York (all other counties), Connecticut, Maine, Massachusetts, New Hampshire, Rhode Island, Vermont	P.O. Box 371999 Pittsburgh, PA 15250-7999
Delaware, District of Columbia, Maryland, Pennsylvania, Virginia	P.O. Box 8318 Philadelphia, PA 19162-8318
Florida, Georgia, South Carolina	P.O. Box 105900 Atlanta, GA 30348-5900
Indiana, Kentucky, Michigan, Ohio, West Virginia	P.O. Box 7422 Chicago, IL 60680-7422
Alabama, Arkansas, Louisiana, Mississippi, North Carolina, Tennessee	P.O. Box 1219 Charlotte, NC 28201-1219
Illinois, Iowa, Minnesota, Missouri, Wisconsin	P.O. Box 970006 St. Louis, MO 63197-0006
Kansas, New Mexico, Oklahoma, Texas	P.O. Box 970001 St. Louis, MO 63197-0001
Alaska, Arizona, California (counties of Alpine, Amador, Butte, Calaveras, Colusa, Contra Costa, Del Norte, El Dorado, Glenn, Humboldt, Lake, Lassen, Marin, Mendocino, Modoc, Napa, Nevada, Placer, Plumas, Sacramento, San Joaquin, Shasta, Sierra, Siskiyou, Solano, Sonoma, Sutter, Tehama, Trinity, Yolo, and Yuba), Colorado, Idaho, Montana, Nebraska, Nevada, North Dakota, Oregon, South Dakota, Utah, Washington, Wyoming	P.O. Box 510000 San Francisco, CA 94151-5100
California (all other counties), Hawaii	P.O. Box 54030 Los Angeles, CA 90054-0030
American Samoa	P.O. Box 8318 Philadelphia, PA 19162-8318
The Commonwealth of the Northern Mariana Islands	P.O. Box 8318 Philadelphia, PA 19162-8318
Puerto Rico (or if excluding income under section 933)	P.O. Box 8318 Philadelphia, PA 19162-8318
Guam: Nonpermanent residents	P.O. Box 8318 Philadelphia, PA 19162-8318
Permanent residents*	Department of Revenue and Taxation Government of Guam P.O. Box 23607 GMF, GU 96921

* You must prepare separate vouchers for estimated income tax and self-employment tax payments. Send the income tax vouchers to the Guam address and the self-employment tax vouchers to the address for Guam nonpermanent residents shown above.

Virgin Islands: Nonpermanent residents	P.O. Box 8318 Philadelphia, PA 19162-8318
Permanent residents*	V.I. Bureau of Internal Revenue 9601 Estate Thomas Charlotte Amalie St. Thomas, VI 00802

* You must prepare separate vouchers for estimated income tax and self-employment tax payments. Send the income tax vouchers to the Virgin Islands address and the self-employment tax vouchers to the address for Virgin Islands nonpermanent residents shown above.

All APO and FPO addresses	P.O. Box 8318 Philadelphia, PA 19162-8318
Foreign country: U.S. citizens and those filing Form 2555, Form 2555-EZ, or Form 4563	P.O. Box 8318 Philadelphia, PA 19162-8318

Form 1040-ES - Estimated Tax (Page 7)

Form 1040-ES
Department of the Treasury
Internal Revenue Service

1998 Payment Voucher 3

OMB No. 1545-0087

File only if you are making a payment of estimated tax. Return this voucher with check or money order payable to the "**Internal Revenue Service.**" Please write your social security number and "1998 Form 1040-ES" on your check or money order. Do not send cash. Enclose, but do not staple or attach, your payment with this voucher.

Calendar year—Due Sept. 15, 1998

Amount of payment

$ ....

Please type or print

Your first name and initial	Your last name	Your social security number
If joint payment, complete for spouse		
Spouse's first name and initial	Spouse's last name	Spouse's social security number
Address (number, street, and apt. no.)		
City, state, and ZIP code (If a foreign address, enter city, province or state, postal code, and country.)		

For Paperwork Reduction Act Notice, see instructions on page 5.

------ Tear off here ------

Form 1040-ES
Department of the Treasury
Internal Revenue Service

1998 Payment Voucher 2

OMB No. 1545-0087

File only if you are making a payment of estimated tax. Return this voucher with check or money order payable to the "**Internal Revenue Service.**" Please write your social security number and "1998 Form 1040-ES" on your check or money order. Do not send cash. Enclose, but do not staple or attach, your payment with this voucher.

Calendar year—Due June 15, 1998

Amount of payment

$ ....

Please type or print

Your first name and initial	Your last name	Your social security number
If joint payment, complete for spouse		
Spouse's first name and initial	Spouse's last name	Spouse's social security number
Address (number, street, and apt. no.)		
City, state, and ZIP code (If a foreign address, enter city, province or state, postal code, and country.)		

For Paperwork Reduction Act Notice, see instructions on page 5.

------ Tear off here ------

Form 1040-ES
Department of the Treasury
Internal Revenue Service

1998 Payment Voucher 1

OMB No. 1545-0087

File only if you are making a payment of estimated tax. Return this voucher with check or money order payable to the "**Internal Revenue Service.**" Please write your social security number and "1998 Form 1040-ES" on your check or money order. Do not send cash. Enclose, but do not staple or attach, your payment with this voucher.

Calendar year—Due April 15, 1998

Amount of payment

$ ....

Please type or print

Your first name and initial	Your last name	Your social security number
If joint payment, complete for spouse		
Spouse's first name and initial	Spouse's last name	Spouse's social security number
Address (number, street, and apt. no.)		
City, state, and ZIP code (If a foreign address, enter city, province or state, postal code, and country.)		

For Paperwork Reduction Act Notice, see instructions on page 5.

Appendix D – IRS Tax Forms

Form 4562 - Depreciation and Amortization (Front)

Form 4562 — Depreciation and Amortization (Including Information on Listed Property)
Department of the Treasury — Internal Revenue Service (U)
▶ See separate instructions. ▶ Attach this form to your return.

OMB No. 1545-0172
1997
Attachment Sequence No. 67

Name(s) shown on return | Business or activity to which this form relates | Identifying number

Part I — Election To Expense Certain Tangible Property (Section 179) (Note: If you have any "listed property," complete Part V before you complete Part I.)

1. Maximum dollar limitation. If an enterprise zone business, see page 2 of the instructions . . **1** $18,000
2. Total cost of section 179 property placed in service. See page 2 of the instructions **2**
3. Threshold cost of section 179 property before reduction in limitation **3** $200,000
4. Reduction in limitation. Subtract line 3 from line 2. If zero or less, enter -0- **4**
5. Dollar limitation for tax year. Subtract line 4 from line 1. If zero or less, enter -0-. If married filing separately, see page 2 of the instructions **5**

(a) Description of property	(b) Cost (business use only)	(c) Elected cost
6		

7. Listed property. Enter amount from line 27 . . . . **7**
8. Total elected cost of section 179 property. Add amounts in column (c), lines 6 and 7 . . . **8**
9. Tentative deduction. Enter the smaller of line 5 or line 8 . . . . **9**
10. Carryover of disallowed deduction from 1996. See page 3 of the instructions **10**
11. Business income limitation. Enter the smaller of business income (not less than zero) or line 5 (see instructions) **11**
12. Section 179 expense deduction. Add lines 9 and 10, but do not enter more than line 11 . . **12**
13. Carryover of disallowed deduction to 1998. Add lines 9 and 10, less line 12 ▶ **13**

Note: *Do not use Part II or Part III below for listed property (automobiles, certain other vehicles, cellular telephones, certain computers, or property used for entertainment, recreation, or amusement). Instead, use Part V for listed property.*

Part II — MACRS Depreciation For Assets Placed in Service ONLY During Your 1997 Tax Year (Do Not Include Listed Property.)

Section A—General Asset Account Election

14. If you are making the election under section 168(i)(4) to group any assets placed in service during the tax year into one or more general asset accounts, check this box. See page 3 of the instructions . . . . ▶ ☐

Section B—General Depreciation System (GDS) (See page 3 of the instructions.)

(a) Classification of property	(b) Month and year placed in service	(c) Basis for depreciation (business/investment use only—see instructions)	(d) Recovery period	(e) Convention	(f) Method	(g) Depreciation deduction
15a 3-year property						
b 5-year property						
c 7-year property						
d 10-year property						
e 15-year property						
f 20-year property						
g 25-year property			25 yrs.		S/L	
h Residential rental property			27.5 yrs.	MM	S/L	
			27.5 yrs.	MM	S/L	
i Nonresidential real property			39 yrs.	MM	S/L	
				MM	S/L	

Section C—Alternative Depreciation System (ADS) (See page 6 of the instructions.)

16a Class life					S/L	
b 12-year			12 yrs.		S/L	
c 40-year			40 yrs.	MM	S/L	

Part III — Other Depreciation (Do Not Include Listed Property.) (See page 6 of the instructions.)

17. GDS and ADS deductions for assets placed in service in tax years beginning before 1997 . . . . **17**
18. Property subject to section 168(f)(1) election **18**
19. ACRS and other depreciation **19**

Part IV — Summary (See page 7 of the instructions.)

20. Listed property. Enter amount from line 26 . . . . **20**
21. Total. Add deductions on line 12, lines 15 and 16 in column (g), and lines 17 through 20. Enter here and on the appropriate lines of your return. Partnerships and S corporations—see instructions . . **21**
22. For assets shown above and placed in service during the current year, enter the portion of the basis attributable to section 263A costs **22**

For Paperwork Reduction Act Notice, see the separate instructions. Cat. No. 15789Q Form **4562** (1997)

Form 4562 - Depreciation and Amortization (Back)

Form 4562 (1997) — Page 2

Part V — Listed Property—Automobiles, Certain Other Vehicles, Cellular Telephones, Certain Computers, and Property Used for Entertainment, Recreation, or Amusement

Note: *For any vehicle for which you are using the standard mileage rate or deducting lease expense, complete **only** 23a, 23b, columns (a) through (c) of Section A, all of Section B, and Section C if applicable.*

Section A—Depreciation and Other Information (Caution: *See page 8 of the instructions for limits for passenger automobiles.*)

23a Do you have evidence to support the business/investment use claimed? ☐ Yes ☐ No   23b If "Yes," is the evidence written? ☐ Yes ☐ No

(a) Type of property (list vehicles first)	(b) Date placed in service	(c) Business/investment use percentage	(d) Cost or other basis	(e) Basis for depreciation (business/investment use only)	(f) Recovery period	(g) Method/Convention	(h) Depreciation deduction	(i) Elected section 179 cost

24 Property used more than 50% in a qualified business use (See page 7 of the instructions.):

		%						
		%						
		%						

25 Property used 50% or less in a qualified business use (See page 7 of the instructions.):

		%				S/L –		
		%				S/L –		
		%				S/L –		

26 Add amounts in column (h). Enter the total here and on line 20, page 1 26

27 Add amounts in column (i). Enter the total here and on line 7, page 1 27

Section B—Information on Use of Vehicles

Complete this section for vehicles used by a sole proprietor, partner, or other "more than 5% owner," or related person.
If you provided vehicles to your employees, first answer the questions in Section C to see if you meet an exception to completing this section for those vehicles.

		(a) Vehicle 1	(b) Vehicle 2	(c) Vehicle 3	(d) Vehicle 4	(e) Vehicle 5	(f) Vehicle 6
28	Total business/investment miles driven during the year (DO NOT include commuting miles)						
29	Total commuting miles driven during the year						
30	Total other personal (noncommuting) miles driven						
31	Total miles driven during the year. Add lines 28 through 30.						

		Yes	No	Yes	No	Yes	No	Yes	No	Yes	No	Yes	No
32	Was the vehicle available for personal use during off-duty hours?												
33	Was the vehicle used primarily by a more than 5% owner or related person?												
34	Is another vehicle available for personal use?												

Section C—Questions for Employers Who Provide Vehicles for Use by Their Employees

Answer these questions to determine if you meet an exception to completing Section B for vehicles used by employees who **are not** more than 5% owners or related persons.

		Yes	No
35	Do you maintain a written policy statement that prohibits all personal use of vehicles, including commuting, by your employees?		
36	Do you maintain a written policy statement that prohibits personal use of vehicles, except commuting, by your employees? See page 9 of the instructions for vehicles used by corporate officers, directors, or 1% or more owners		
37	Do you treat all use of vehicles by employees as personal use?		
38	Do you provide more than five vehicles to your employees, obtain information from your employees about the use of the vehicles, and retain the information received?		
39	Do you meet the requirements concerning qualified automobile demonstration use? See page 9 of the instructions . .		

Note: *If your answer to 35, 36, 37, 38, or 39 is "Yes," you need not complete Section B for the covered vehicles.*

Part VI Amortization

(a) Description of costs	(b) Date amortization begins	(c) Amortizable amount	(d) Code section	(e) Amortization period or percentage	(f) Amortization for this year

40 Amortization of costs that begins during your 1997 tax year:

| | | | | | |
| | | | | | |

41 Amortization of costs that began before 1997 41

42 **Total.** Enter here and on "Other Deductions" or "Other Expenses" line of your return . . . 42

Appendix D – IRS Tax Forms

Form 8829 - Expenses for Business Use of Your Home

Form 8829
Department of the Treasury
Internal Revenue Service (O)

Expenses for Business Use of Your Home
▶ File only with Schedule C (Form 1040). Use a separate Form 8829 for each home you used for business during the year.
▶ See separate instructions.

OMB No. 1545-1266
1997
Attachment Sequence No. 66

Name(s) of proprietor(s) — Your social security number

Part I — Part of Your Home Used for Business

1. Area used regularly and exclusively for business, regularly for day care, or for storage of inventory or product samples. See instructions 1
2. Total area of home 2
3. Divide line 1 by line 2. Enter the result as a percentage . . . . 3 %
   - For day-care facilities not used exclusively for business, also complete lines 4–6.
   - All others, skip lines 4–6 and enter the amount from line 3 on line 7.
4. Multiply days used for day care during year by hours used per day . 4 _____ hr.
5. Total hours available for use during the year (365 days × 24 hours). See instructions 5 8,760 hr.
6. Divide line 4 by line 5. Enter the result as a decimal amount . . . 6 .
7. Business percentage. For day-care facilities not used exclusively for business, multiply line 6 by line 3 (enter the result as a percentage). All others, enter the amount from line 3 . . . . ▶ 7 %

Part II — Figure Your Allowable Deduction

8. Enter the amount from Schedule C, line 29, **plus** any net gain or (loss) derived from the business use of your home and shown on Schedule D or Form 4797. If more than one place of business, see instructions . . . 8

See instructions for columns (a) and (b) before completing lines 9–20.

		(a) Direct expenses	(b) Indirect expenses
9	Casualty losses. See instructions		
10	Deductible mortgage interest. See instructions		
11	Real estate taxes. See instructions		
12	Add lines 9, 10, and 11		
13	Multiply line 12, column (b) by line 7		13

14. Add line 12, column (a) and line 13 14
15. Subtract line 14 from line 8. If zero or less, enter -0- 15

16	Excess mortgage interest. See instructions		
17	Insurance		
18	Repairs and maintenance		
19	Utilities		
20	Other expenses. See instructions		
21	Add lines 16 through 20		
22	Multiply line 21, column (b) by line 7		22
23	Carryover of operating expenses from 1996 Form 8829, line 41		23

24. Add line 21 in column (a), line 22, and line 23 24
25. Allowable operating expenses. Enter the **smaller** of line 15 or line 24 25
26. Limit on excess casualty losses and depreciation. Subtract line 25 from line 15 26

27	Excess casualty losses. See instructions	
28	Depreciation of your home from Part III below	28
29	Carryover of excess casualty losses and depreciation from 1996 Form 8829, line 42	29

30. Add lines 27 through 29 30
31. Allowable excess casualty losses and depreciation. Enter the **smaller** of line 26 or line 30 . . 31
32. Add lines 14, 25, and 31 32
33. Casualty loss portion, if any, from lines 14 and 31. Carry amount to **Form 4684**, Section B . 33
34. Allowable expenses for business use of your home. Subtract line 33 from line 32. Enter here and on Schedule C, line 30. If your home was used for more than one business, see instructions ▶ 34

Part III — Depreciation of Your Home

35. Enter the **smaller** of your home's adjusted basis or its fair market value. See instructions . . 35
36. Value of land included on line 35 36
37. Basis of building. Subtract line 36 from line 35 37
38. Business basis of building. Multiply line 37 by line 7 38
39. Depreciation percentage. See instructions . . . . 39 %
40. Depreciation allowable. Multiply line 38 by line 39. Enter here and on line 28 above. See instructions 40

Part IV — Carryover of Unallowed Expenses to 1998

41. Operating expenses. Subtract line 25 from line 24. If less than zero, enter -0- 41
42. Excess casualty losses and depreciation. Subtract line 31 from line 30. If less than zero, enter -0- 42

For Paperwork Reduction Act Notice, see page 3 of separate instructions.   Printed on recycled paper   Cat. No. 13232M   Form **8829** (1997)

Form 1128-Application to Adopt, Change, or Retain a Tax Year (Page 1)

Form 1128
(Rev. April 1996)
Department of the Treasury
Internal Revenue Service

Application To Adopt, Change, or Retain a Tax Year

▶ Instructions are separate.

OMB No. 1545-0134

Part I — General Information (All applicants complete this part. See page 4 for required signature(s). Also see page 2 of the instructions.)

Please Type or Print	
Name of applicant (If a joint return is filed, also give spouse's name.)	Identifying number (See page 2 of the instructions.)
Number, street, and room or suite no. (If a P.O. box, see page 2 of the instructions.)	Service center where income tax return will be filed
City or town, state, and ZIP code	Applicant's area code and telephone number/Fax number ( ) / ( )
Name of person to contact (If not the applicant, attach a power of attorney.)	Contact person's area code and telephone number/Fax number ( ) / ( )

1 Check the appropriate box to indicate who is filing this form.

☐ Individual   ☐ Personal Service Corporation   ☐ Specified Foreign Corporation (Sec. 898)
☐ Partnership   ☐ Cooperative (Sec. 1381(a))   ☐ Passive Foreign Investment Company (Sec. 1296)
☐ Estate   ☐ Possession Corporation (Sec. 936)   ☐ Other Foreign Corporation
☐ Corporation   ☐ Controlled Foreign Corporation (Sec. 957) ☐ Tax-Exempt Organization
☐ S Corporation   ☐ Foreign Personal Holding Company (Sec. 552) ☐ Other ....
                                                                        (Specify entity and applicable Code section)

2a Approval is requested to (check one) (see page 2 of the instructions):

☐ Adopt a tax year ending ▶..
(Partnerships and personal service corporations: Go to Part III after completing Part I.)

☐ Change to a tax year ending ▶..

☐ Retain a tax year ending ▶..

b If changing a tax year, indicate the date the present tax year ends. ▶..........................

c If adopting or changing a tax year, indicate the short period return that will be required to be filed for the tax year beginning ▶ _____, 19____, and ending ▶ _____, 19____

3 Is the applicant using the same tax year for both Federal income tax and financial reporting purposes? ▶ ☐ Yes ☐ No

4 Indicate the applicant's present overall method of accounting.

☐ Cash receipts and disbursements method

☐ Accrual method

☐ Other method (specify) ▶

5 State the nature of the applicant's business or principal source of income.

_____

6 Is **Form 2848**, Power of Attorney and Declaration of Representative, attached to this application? . ▶ ☐ Yes ☐ No

7 Does the applicant request a **conference of right** at the IRS National Office? (See page 2 of the instructions.) . . . . ▶ ☐ Yes ☐ No

8 Enter amount of **user fee** attached to this application. (See page 2 of the instructions.) . . . . . . ▶ $

For Paperwork Reduction Act Notice, see separate instructions.   Cat. No. 21115C   Form **1128** (Rev. 4-96)

Appendix D – IRS Tax Forms

Form 1128-Application to Adopt, Change, or Retain a Tax Year (Page 2)

Form 1128 (Rev. 4-96)   Page **2**

Part II — Expeditious Approval Requests
(If the answer to any of the questions below is "Yes," file Form 1128 with the IRS service center where the applicant's income tax return is filed. **Do not** include a user fee. See pages 2 and 3 of the instructions.)

		Yes	No
1	**Rev. Proc. 92-13.**—Is the applicant a corporation described in section 4 of Rev. Proc. 92-13, 1992-1 C.B. 665 (as modified by Rev. Proc. 94-12, 1994-1 C.B. 565, and as modified and amplified by Rev. Proc. 92-13A, 1992-1 C.B. 668), that is requesting a change in a tax year under Rev. Proc. 92-13? ▶		
2a	**Rev. Proc. 87-32.**—Is the applicant a partnership, an S corporation, or a personal service corporation that is requesting a tax year under the expeditious approval rules in section 4 of Rev. Proc. 87-32, 1987-2 C.B. 396, but is not precluded from using the expeditious approval rules under section 3 of that revenue procedure? ▶		
b	Is the applicant a partnership, an S corporation, or a personal service corporation that is requesting a tax year that coincides with its natural business year as defined in section 4.01(1) of Rev. Proc. 87-32, **and** the tax year results in no greater deferral of income to the partners or shareholders than the present tax year? ▶		
c	Is the applicant an S corporation whose shareholders own more than 50% of the shares of the corporation's stock (as of the first day of the tax year to which the request relates) **and** the shareholders have the same tax year the corporation is requesting? ▶		
d	Is the applicant an S corporation whose shareholders own more than 50% of the shares of the corporation's stock (as of the first day of the tax year to which the request relates) **and** the shareholders have requested approval to concurrently change to the tax year that the corporation is requesting? ▶		
3	**Rev. Proc. 66-50.**—Is the applicant an individual requesting a change from a fiscal year to a calendar year under Rev. Proc. 66-50, 1966-2 C.B. 1260? ▶		
4	**Rev. Proc. 85-58 or 76-10.**—Is the applicant a tax-exempt organization requesting a change under Rev. Proc. 85-58, 1985-2 C.B. 740, or Rev. Proc. 76-10, 1976-1 C.B. 548? ▶		

Part III — Ruling Requests
(All applicants requesting a ruling must complete Section A and any other specific section that applies to the entity. See page 4 of the instructions.)

SECTION A—General Information (See page 4 of the instructions.)

		Yes	No
1a	In the last 6 years has the applicant changed or requested approval to change its tax year? ▶ If "Yes" and a ruling letter was issued granting approval to make the change, attach a copy of the ruling. If a copy of the ruling letter is not available, attach an explanation and give the date the approval was granted. If a ruling letter was not issued, explain the facts and give the date the change was implemented. If the requested change was denied or not implemented, attach an explanation.		
b	If a change in tax year was granted within the last 6 years, attach an explanation discussing why another change in tax year is necessary fully describing any unusual circumstances. (Subsidiaries see page 4 of the instructions.)		
2	Does the applicant have any accounting method, tax year, ruling, or technical advice request pending with the National Office? ▶ If "Yes," attach a statement explaining the type of request (method, tax year, etc.) and the specific issues involved in each request.		
3	Enter the taxable income * or (loss) for the 3 tax years immediately before the short period and for the short period. If necessary, estimate the amount for the short period. Short period $ .... First preceding year $ .... Second preceding year $ .... Third preceding year $ .... *Individuals enter adjusted gross income. Partnerships and S corporations enter ordinary income. Section 501(c) organizations enter unrelated business taxable income. Estates enter adjusted total income. All other applicants enter taxable income before net operating loss deduction and special deductions.		
4	Is the applicant a U.S. shareholder in a controlled foreign corporation (CFC)? ▶ If "Yes," attach a statement for each CFC providing the name, address, identifying number, tax year, the percentage of total combined voting power of the applicant, and the amount of income included in the gross income of the applicant under section 951 for the 3 tax years immediately before the short period and for the short period. Also indicate if the CFC will concurrently change its tax year to comply with section 898 if the applicant's request is granted.		

Form 1128-Application to Adopt, Change, or Retain a Tax Year (Page 3)

Form 1128 (Rev 4-96)   Page **3**

SECTION A—General Information (See page 4 of the instructions.) *(Continued from page 2.)*

		Yes	No
5a	Is the applicant a U.S. shareholder in a passive foreign investment company as defined in section 1296? ▶ If "Yes," attach a statement providing the name, address, identifying number and tax year of the passive foreign investment company, the percentage of interest owned by the applicant, and the amount of ordinary earnings and net capital gain from the passive foreign investment company included in the income of the applicant.		
b	Did the applicant elect under section 1295 to treat the passive foreign investment company as a qualified electing fund? ▶		
6	Is the applicant a member of a partnership, a beneficiary of a trust or estate, a shareholder of an S corporation, a shareholder of an Interest Charge Domestic International Sales Corporation (IC-DISC) or a shareholder in a Foreign Sales Corporation (FSC)? . . . . ▶ If "Yes," attach a statement providing the name, address, identifying number, type of entity (partnership, trust, estate, S corporation, IC-DISC, or FSC), tax year, percentage of interest in capital and profits, or percentage of interest of each IC-DISC and the amount of income received from each partnership, trust, estate, S corporation, IC-DISC, or FSC for the first preceding year and for the short period. Indicate the percentage of gross income of the applicant represented by each amount. Also indicate any partnership that will concurrently change its tax year to comply with section 706 if the applicant's request is granted.		
7	Attach an explanation providing the reasons for requesting the change in tax year. This explanation is required by Regulations section 1.442-1(b)(1). If the reasons are not provided, the application will be denied. (If requesting a ruling based on a natural business year, see page 4 of the instructions.) **Note:** *Corporations that want to elect S corporation status should see line 2 in Section B below and the related instructions.*		

SECTION B—Corporations (other than S corporations and controlled foreign corporations) (See page 4 of the instructions.)

		Yes	No
1	Enter the date of incorporation. ▶		
2	Does the corporation intend to elect to be an S corporation for the tax year immediately following the short period? . . . . ▶ If "Yes," see the instructions on page 4 for restrictions on this election.		
3	Is the corporation a member of an affiliated group filing a consolidated return? . . . . ▶ If "Yes," attach a statement providing **(a)** the name, address, identifying number used on the consolidated return, the tax year, and the Internal Revenue service center where the applicant files the return, **(b)** the name, address, and identifying number of each member of the affiliated group, **(c)** the taxable income (loss) of each member for the 3 years immediately before the short period and for the short period, and **(d)** the name of the parent corporation.		
4	Personal service corporations:		
a	Attach a statement providing each shareholder's name, type of entity (e.g., individual, partnership, corporation, etc.), address, identifying number, tax year, and percentage of ownership.		
b	If the corporation is using a tax year other than the required tax year, indicate how it obtained its tax year (i.e., "grandfathered," section 444 election, or ruling from the IRS National Office). ▶		
c	If the corporation received a ruling, indicate the date of the ruling and provide a copy of the ruling letter. ▶		
d	If the corporation made a section 444 election, indicate the date of the election. ▶		

SECTION C—S Corporations (See page 4 of the instructions.)

		Yes	No
1	Enter the date of the S corporation election. ▶		
2	Is any shareholder applying for a corresponding change in tax year? . . . . ▶		
3a	If the corporation is using a tax year other than the required tax year, indicate how it obtained its tax year (i.e., "grandfathered," section 444 election, or ruling from the IRS National Office). ▶		
b	If the corporation received a ruling, indicate the date of the ruling and provide a copy of the ruling letter. ▶		
c	If the corporation made a section 444 election, indicate the date of the election. ▶		
4	Attach a statement providing each shareholder's name, type of entity (i.e., individual, estate, trust, or qualified Subchapter S Trust as defined in section 1361(d)(3)), address, identifying number, tax year, and percentage of ownership.		

Appendix D – IRS Tax Forms

Form 1128-Application to Adopt, Change, or Retain a Tax Year (Page 4)

Form 1128 (Rev. 4-96)   Page **4**

SECTION D—Partnerships (See page 4 of the instructions.)   Yes | No

1. Enter the date the partnership's business began. ▶
2. Is any partner applying for a corresponding change in tax year? . . . . ▶
3. Attach a statement providing each partner's name, type of partner (e.g., individual, partnership, estate, trust, corporation, S corporation, IC-DISC, etc.), address, identifying number, tax year, and the percentage of interest in capital and profits.
4. Is any partner a shareholder of a personal service corporation as defined in Temporary Regulations section 1.441-4T(d)(1)? . . . . ▶
   If "Yes," attach a statement providing the name, address, identifying number, tax year, percentage of interest in capital and profits, and the amount of income received from each personal service corporation for the first preceding year and for the short period.
5a. If the partnership is using a tax year other than the required tax year, indicate how it obtained its tax year (i.e., "grandfathered," section 444 election, or ruling from the IRS National Office). ▶ ....
   b. If the partnership received a ruling, indicate the date of the ruling and provide a copy of the ruling letter. ▶ ....
   c. If the partnership made a section 444 election, indicate the date of the election. ▶

SECTION E—Controlled Foreign Corporations (See page 4 of the instructions.)   Yes | No

1. Attach a statement for each U.S. shareholder (as defined in section 951(b)) providing the name, address, identifying number, tax year, percentage of total combined voting power, and the amount of income included in gross income under section 951 for the 3 tax years immediately before the short period and for the short period.
2. Is the applicant a specified foreign corporation requesting a revocation of its election that was made under section 898(c)(1)(B)? . . . . ▶

SECTION F—Tax-Exempt Organizations   Yes | No

1. Enter the form of organization: ☐ Corporation   ☐ Trust   ☐ Other (specify) ▶
2. Enter the date of organization. ▶
3. Enter the Code section under which the organization is exempt. ▶
4. Is the organization required to file an annual return on Form 990, 990-C, 990-PF, 990-T, 1120-H, or 1120-POL? . . . . ▶
5. Enter the date the exemption was granted. ▶ .... Attach a copy of the ruling letter granting exemption. If a copy of the letter is not available, attach an explanation.
6. If the organization is a private foundation, is the foundation terminating its status under section 507? . . ▶

SECTION G—Estates

1. Enter the date the estate was created. ▶
2. Attach a statement providing:
   a. Name, identifying number, address, and tax year of each beneficiary and each person who is an owner or treated as an owner of any portion of the estate.
   b. Based on the adjusted total income of the estate entered in Part III, Section A, line 3, show the distribution deduction and the taxable amounts distributed to each beneficiary for the 2 tax years immediately before the short period and for the short period.

SECTION H—Passive Foreign Investment Company

Attach a statement providing each U.S. shareholder's name, address, identifying number, and the percentage of interest owned.

Signature—All Applicants (See page 4 of the instructions.)

Under penalties of perjury, I declare that I have examined this application, including accompanying schedules and statements, and to the best of my knowledge and belief it is true, correct, and complete. Declaration of preparer (other than applicant) is based on all information of which preparer has any knowledge.

_____   _____
Applicant's name (print or type)   Date

_____   _____
Applicant's signature (officer of parent corporation, if applicable)   Title

_____   _____
Signing official's name (print or type)   Date

_____   _____
Signature of individual (other than applicant) preparing the application   Date

_____
Firm or preparer's name (print or type)

Printed on recycled paper   *U.S. Government Printing Office: 1996 - 405-493/40126

Organize Your Books in 6 Easy Steps

Form 3115 - Application for Change in Accounting Method (page 1)

Form 3115
(Rev. February 1996)
Department of the Treasury
Internal Revenue Service

Application for Change in Accounting Method

▶ See page 1 of the instructions for Automatic Change Procedures.

OMB No. 1545-0152

Name of applicant (If joint return is filed, also give spouse's name.)	Identifying number (See page 2 of the instructions.)
Number, street, and room or suite no. (If a P.O. box, see page 2 of the instructions.)	Due date for filing Form 3115
City or town, state, and ZIP code	District director's office having jurisdiction
Name of person to contact (If not the applicant, a power of attorney must be submitted.)	Contact person's telephone number/Fax number ( ) / ( )

Check the appropriate box to indicate who is filing this form.
- ☐ Individual
- ☐ Corporation
- ☐ Cooperative (Sec. 1381)
- ☐ Qualified Personal Service Corporation (Sec. 448(d)(2))
- ☐ Exempt organization. Enter code section ▶
- ☐ Partnership
- ☐ S Corporation
- ☐ Insurance Co. (Sec. 816(a))
- ☐ Insurance Co. (Sec. 831)
- ☐ Other (specify) ▶ ....

Check the appropriate box to indicate the type of accounting method change being requested. (See page 2 of the instructions.)
- ☐ Depreciation or Amortization
- ☐ Financial Products and/or Financial Activities of Financial Institutions
- ☐ Other (specify) ▶

Part I Eligibility To Request Change (All applicants complete Parts I through IV unless otherwise indicated.)

		Yes	No
1	Is the applicant changing its method of accounting under a revenue procedure or other published IRS document that provides for automatic changes? (See page 1 of the instructions.) . . . . If "Yes," enter the citation of the revenue procedure or the title of the applicable document. ▶		
2a	Is the applicant a member of an affiliated group filing a consolidated return for the year of change? . . . . . . If "Yes," attach the parent corporation's (1) name, (2) identifying number, (3) address, and (4) tax year. If "No," go to line 3a.		
b	Do all other members of the affiliated group use the method of accounting being requested on this application? . . If "No," attach an explanation.		
3a	Prior to submitting Form 3115, has the applicant, or any member of the affiliated group that has been included in a consolidated return with the applicant, been contacted by the IRS to schedule an examination of any of its Federal income tax returns, or was an examination in process? See section 3.02 of Rev. Proc. 92-20, 1992-1 C.B. 685 . . If "Yes," complete lines 3b and 3c.		
b	Indicate the "window period" referred to in section 6 of Rev. Proc. 92-20 that applies, or state if the change is being requested with the consent of the district director under section 6.06. ▶		
c	Has a copy of this Form 3115 been provided to the district director? See section 10.06 of Rev. Proc. 92-20 . . .		
4a	Does the applicant have any Federal income tax returns under consideration by an appeals office? See section 4.02 of Rev. Proc. 92-20		
b	If "Yes," has the applicant attached the required statement from the appeals officer?		
5a	Does the applicant have any Federal income tax returns under consideration before any Federal court? See section 4.03 of Rev. Proc. 92-20		
b	If "Yes," has the applicant attached the required statement from counsel for the Government?		
6	Is this the first tax year the applicant is required to change its method of accounting under the Internal Revenue Code or regulations? (i.e., sections 263A, 447, 448, 460, or 585) . . . . If "Yes," enter the applicable section. ▶		

Signature—All Applicants (See page 2 of the instructions.)

Under penalties of perjury, I declare that I have examined this application, including accompanying schedules and statements, and to the best of my knowledge and belief, it is true, correct, and complete. Declaration of preparer (other than applicant) is based on all information of which preparer has any knowledge.

Applicant	Parent corporation (if applicable)
....	....
Officer's signature and date	Parent officer's signature and date
....	....
Name and title (print or type)	Name and title (print or type)
....	....
Signature(s) of individual or firm preparing the application and date	Name of firm preparing the application

For Paperwork Reduction Act Notice, see page 1 of the instructions.   Cat. No. 19280E   Form **3115** (Rev. 2-96)

Form 3115 - Application for Change in Accounting Method (page 2)

Form 3115 (Rev. 2-96)   Page 2

Part II — Description of Change

7. Enter the gross receipts for the 4 tax years preceding the year of change. (See page 2 of the instructions.)
   $ .... $ .... $ .... $ ....
8. Tax year of change begins (month, day, year) ▶ .... and ends (month, day, year) ▶ ....
9. Is the applicant applying to change its **overall** method of accounting?.
   If "Yes," check appropriate boxes below to indicate the applicant's present and proposed methods of accounting. Also complete Schedule A on page 3.
   Present method: ☐ Cash   ☐ Accrual   ☐ Other (attach description)
   Proposed method: ☐ Cash   ☐ Accrual   ☐ Other (attach description)
10. If the applicant is **not** changing its overall method of accounting, attach a description of each of the following:
    a. The item(s) being changed.
    b. The applicant's present method for the item being changed.
    c. The applicant's proposed method for the item being changed.
    d. The applicant's overall method of accounting.
    - **Applicants filing under an automatic change procedure:** Skip lines 11 through 19 and go to line 20.
11. Attach an explanation of the legal basis supporting the proposed change. Include all authority (statutes, regulations, published rulings, court cases, etc.) supporting the proposed change. The applicant is encouraged to include a discussion of any authorities that may be contrary to the proposed change in method of accounting.
12. Attach a statement of the applicant's reasons for the proposed change.
13. Attach a copy of all documents directly related to the proposed change. (See page 2 of the instructions.)
14. Attach an explanation of whether the proposed method of accounting conforms to generally accepted accounting principles (GAAP) and state whether the proposed method will be used for financial accounting purposes, including financial statements. (Insurance companies, see page 2 of the instructions.)
15. Does the applicant assert that its present method is a Category A method as defined in section 3.06 of Rev. Proc. 92-20?.
    If "Yes," attach a statement giving the legal basis for the determination.
16. Is the applicant's present method a "Designated B" method as defined in section 3.09 of Rev. Proc. 92-20? (See page 2 of the instructions.)
    If "Yes," enter the title of the designating document. ▶ ....
17. Attach a description of the applicant's trade or business, operations, goods and services, and any other types of activities generating gross income.
18. a. Does the applicant have more than one trade or business as defined in Regulations section 1.446-1(d)?.
    b. If "Yes," is each trade or business accounted for separately?
    If "Yes," for each trade or business attach a description of the type of business, the overall method of accounting, whether the business has changed its accounting method in the last 6 years, and whether the business is changing its accounting method as part of this application or as a separate application.
19. Attach a statement addressing whether the applicant has entered (or is considering entering) into a transaction (for example, a reorganization or merger) to which section 381(c)(4) or (5) applies during the tax year of change. Also include in the statement an explanation of any changes in method of accounting that resulted (or will result) from the transaction(s).

Part III — Section 481(a) Adjustment

20. Enter the net section 481(a) adjustment for the year of change. Indicate whether the adjustment is an increase (+) or a decrease (−) in income. ▶ $ ....
21. Enter the adjustment that would have been required if the requested change had been made for the tax year preceding the year of change. Indicate (+) or (−). ▶ $ .... (See page 3 of the instructions.)
22. Is any part of the adjustment attributable to transactions between members of an affiliated group, a controlled group, or other related parties?.
    If "Yes," attach an explanation.
23. Has the adjustment for the year of change been reduced by a pre-1954 amount?.
24. Enter the number of years the present method has been used by the applicant. ▶ .... (See page 3 of the instructions.)
25. Enter the applicable period over which the applicant proposes to take the adjustment into account. ▶ ....
26. If the adjustment for the year of change is less than $25,000, does the applicant elect to take the entire adjustment into account in the year of change?.
27. Enter the NOL, if any, that will expire in the year of change. ▶ $ ....
28. Enter the credit carryover, if any, that will expire in the year of change. ▶ $

Form 3115 - Application for Change in Accounting Method (page 3)

Form 3115 (Rev. 2-96)   Page **3**

Part IV — Additional Information (Applicants filing under an automatic change procedure, skip Part IV.)

		Yes	No
29	Has the applicant, predecessor, or related party requested or made a change in accounting method or accounting period in the past 6 years?		
	If "Yes," attach a description of each change, the year of change, and whether a ruling letter was received. If a ruling letter granting the change was received but the change was not made, include an explanation.		
30	Does the applicant, predecessor, or related party currently have pending any request for a private letter ruling, a request for change in accounting method or accounting period, or a request for technical advice?		
	If "Yes," for each such request, indicate the name(s) of the entity, type of request (method, tax year, etc.) and the specific issue in each request.		
31	Has the applicant attached **Form 2848**, Power of Attorney and Declaration of Representative? (See page 3 of the instructions.)		
32	Does the applicant request a **conference of right** at the IRS National Office if the IRS proposes an adverse response?		
33	Enter the amount of **user fee** attached to this application. ▶ $ _____ (See page 2 of the instructions.)		
34	If the applicant qualifies for a reduced user fee for identical accounting method changes, has the information required by Rev. Proc. 92-90, 1992-2 C.B. 501, been attached?		

Schedule A—Change in Overall Method of Accounting (If Schedule A applies, Part I must be completed.)

Attach copies of the profit and loss statement (Schedule F (Form 1040) for farmers) and the balance sheet, if applicable, as of the close of the tax year preceding the year of change. On a separate sheet, state the accounting method used when preparing the balance sheet. If books of account are not kept, attach a copy of the business schedules submitted with the Federal income tax return or other return (e.g., tax-exempt organization returns) for that period. If the amounts in Part I, lines 1a through 1g, do not agree with those shown on both the profit and loss statement and the balance sheet, explain the differences on a separate sheet.

Part I — Change in Overall Method (See page 3 of the instructions.)

1   Enter the following amounts as of the close of the tax year preceding the year of change. If none, state "None." Also provide a breakdown of the amounts entered on lines 1a through 1g.

		Amount
a	Income accrued but not received	$
b	Income received or reported before it was earned. Attach a description of the income and the legal basis for the proposed method (See page 3 of the instructions.)	
c	Expenses accrued but not paid	
d	Prepaid expense previously deducted	
e	Supplies on hand previously deducted	
f	Inventory on hand previously deducted. Complete Schedule C, Part II.	
g	Other amounts (specify) ▶ _____	
h	Net section 481(a) adjustment (Add lines 1a—1g.) (See page 3 of the instructions.)	$

2   Is the applicant also requesting the recurring item exception (section 461(h)) (See page 3 of the instructions.)? ☐ Yes   ☐ No

Part II — Change to the Cash Method (See page 3 of the instructions.)

Applicants requesting a change to the cash method must attach the following information.

1. A description of the applicant's investment in capital items and leased equipment used in the trade or business, and the relationship between these items and the services performed by the business.
2. A description of inventory items (items that produce income when sold) and materials and supplies used in carrying out the business.
3. The number of employees, shareholders, partners, associates, etc., and a description of their duties in carrying out the applicant's business.
4. A schedule showing the age of receivables for each of the 4 tax years preceding the year of change.
5. A schedule showing the applicant's taxable income (loss) for each of the 4 tax years preceding the year of change.
6. A profit and loss statement showing the taxable income (loss) based on the cash method for each of the 4 tax years preceding the year of change.

Appendix D – IRS Tax Forms

Form 3115 - Application for Change in Accounting Method (page 4)

Form 3115 (Rev. 2-96)   Page 4

Schedule B—Changes Within the LIFO Inventory Method (See page 3 of the instructions.)

Part I — General LIFO Information

Complete this section if the requested change involves changes within the LIFO inventory method. Also, attach a copy of all **Forms 970**, Application to Use LIFO Inventory Method, filed to adopt or expand the use of the LIFO method.

1. Attach a description of the applicant's present and proposed LIFO methods and submethods for each of the following items.
   a. Valuing inventory (i.e., unit method or dollar-value method).
   b. Pooling (e.g., by line or type or class of goods; natural business unit; multiple pools; raw material content; simplified dollar-value method; pooling method authorized under inventory price index (IPI) computation method, etc.).
   c. Pricing dollar-value pools (e.g., double-extension, index, link-chain, link-chain index, IPI computation method, etc.).
   d. Figuring the cost of goods in the closing inventory over the cost of goods in the opening inventory (e.g., most recent purchases, earliest acquisitions during the year, average cost of purchases during the year, etc.).

2. If any present method or submethod used by the applicant is not the same as indicated on Form(s) 970 filed to adopt or expand the use of the method, attach an explanation.

3. If the proposed change is not requested for all the LIFO inventory, specify the inventory to which the change is and is not applicable.

4. If the proposed change is not requested for all of the LIFO pools, specify the pool(s) to which the change is applicable.

5. Attach a statement addressing whether the applicant values any of its LIFO inventory on a method other than cost. For example, if the applicant values some of its LIFO inventory at retail and the remainder at cost, the applicant should identify which inventory items are valued under each method.

Part II — Change in Pooling Inventories

1. If the applicant is proposing to change its pooling method or the number of pools, attach a description of the contents and state the base year for each dollar-value pool the applicant presently uses and proposes to use.

2. If proposing to use natural business unit (NBU) pools or requesting to change the number of NBU pools, attach the following information (to the extent not already provided) in sufficient detail to show that each proposed NBU was determined under Regulations section 1.472-8(b)(1) and (2):
   a. A description of the types of products produced by the applicant. If possible, attach a brochure.
   b. A description of the types of processes and raw materials used to produce the products in each proposed pool.
   c. If all of the products to be included in the proposed NBU pool(s) are not produced at one facility, the applicant should explain the reasons for the separate facilities, indicate the location of each facility, and provide a description of the products each facility produces.
   d. A description of the natural business divisions adopted by the taxpayer. State whether separate cost centers are maintained and if separate profit and loss statements are prepared.
   e. A statement addressing whether the applicant has inventories of items purchased and held for resale that are not further processed by the applicant, including whether such items, if any, will be included in any proposed NBU pool.
   f. A statement addressing whether all items including raw materials, goods-in-process, and finished goods entering into the entire inventory investment for each proposed NBU pool are presently valued under the LIFO method. Describe any items that are not presently valued under the LIFO method that are to be included in each proposed pool.
   g. A statement addressing whether, within the proposed NBU pool(s), there are items sold to others and transferred to a different unit of the applicant to be used as a component part of another product prior to final processing.

3. If the applicant is engaged in manufacturing and is proposing to use the multiple pooling method or raw material content pools, attach information to show that each proposed pool will consist of a group of items that are substantially similar. See Regulations section 1.472-8(b)(3).

4. If the applicant is engaged in the wholesaling or retailing of goods and is requesting to change the number of pools used, attach information to show that each of the proposed pools is based on customary business classifications of the applicant's trade or business.

Part III — Change to Inventory Price Index (IPI) Computation Method (See page 3 of the instructions.)

If changing to the IPI computation method, attach the following items.

1. A completed Form 970.
2. A statement indicating which indexes, tables, and categories the applicant proposes to use.

Form 3115 - Application for Change in Accounting Method (page 5)

Form 3115 (Rev 2-96)   Page **5**

Schedule C—Change in the Treatment of Long-Term Contracts, Inventories, or Other Section 263A Assets

Part I   Change in Reporting Income From Long-Term Contracts (Complete Part I and Part III below. See page 3 of the instructions.)

1. To the extent not already provided, attach a description of the applicant's present and proposed methods for reporting income from long-term contracts. If the applicant is a construction contractor, include a description of its construction activities.

2a. Are the applicant's contracts long-term contracts as defined in section 460(f)(1)? (See page 3 of the instructions.) ☐ Yes ☐ No

  b. If "Yes," do all the contracts qualify for the exception under section 460(e)? (See page 3 of the instructions.) ☐ Yes ☐ No

    If line 2b is "No," attach an explanation.

3a. Does the applicant have long-term manufacturing contracts as defined in section 460(f)(2)? . . . . ☐ Yes ☐ No

  b. If "Yes," explain the applicant's present and proposed method(s) of accounting for long-term manufacturing contracts.

  c. If any of the manufacturing goods are sold or distributed without installation, attach an explanation.

4. If the applicant is requesting to use the percentage of completion method under section 460(b) for reporting its long-term contract income, indicate whether the applicant is electing to determine the completion factor for each long-term contract under the simplified cost-to-cost method. (See page 3 of the instructions.)

5. Does the applicant want to change the accounting method for all long-term contracts that were outstanding at the beginning of the year of change? . . . . ☐ Yes ☐ No

    If "No," attach an explanation.

6. Attach a statement indicating whether any of the applicant's contracts are either cost-plus long-term contracts or Federal long-term contracts.

Part II   Change in Valuing Inventories (Complete Part III if applicable. See page 3 of the instructions.)

1. Attach a description of the inventory goods being changed.

2. Attach a description of the inventory goods (if any) NOT being changed.

3. Does the proposed change involve a change in the treatment of package design costs? (See page 4 of the instructions.) . . . . ☐ Yes ☐ No

4. Is the applicant's present inventory valuation method in compliance with section 263A? (See page 4 of the instructions.) . . . . ☐ Yes ☐ No

5a. Check (✓) the appropriate boxes below that identify the present and proposed inventory identification and valuation methods being changed and the present inventory identification and valuation methods not being changed.

	Inventory Being Changed		Inventory Not Being Changed
	Present method	Proposed method	Present method
Identification methods:			
Specific identification			
FIFO			
LIFO			
Valuation methods:			
Cost			
Cost or market, whichever is lower			
Retail cost			
Retail, lower of cost or market			
Other (attach explanation)			

  b. Enter the value at the end of the tax year preceding the year of change . . . .

6. Attach the computation used to determine the section 481(a) adjustment. If the section 481(a) adjustment is based on more than one component, show the computation for each component.

7. If the applicant is changing from the LIFO inventory method to a non-LIFO method, attach the following information. (See page 4 of the instructions.)

  a. Copies of Form(s) 970 filed to adopt or expand the use of the method.

  b. A statement describing how the proposed method is consistent with the requirements of Regulations section 1.472-6.

  c. The termination event statement required by section 7 of Rev. Proc. 88-15, 1988-1 C.B. 683, or section 9.03 of Rev. Proc. 92-20 (whichever is applicable) and an explanation if there has been a termination event.

Part III   Method of Cost Allocation (See page 4 of the instructions.)

Complete this part if the requested change involves either property subject to section 263A or to long-term contracts subject to section 460. Check (✓) the appropriate boxes in Sections B and C showing which costs, under both the present and proposed methods, are fully included, to the extent required, in the cost of property produced or acquired for resale under section 263A or allocated to long-term contracts under section 460. If a box is not checked, it is assumed that those costs are not fully included to the extent required. If a cost is not fully included, attach an explanation. Mark "N/A" in a box if those costs are not incurred by the applicant with respect to its production, resale, or long-term contract activities.

Appendix D – IRS Tax Forms

Form 3115 - Application for Change in Accounting Method (page 6)

Form 3115 (Rev. 2-96)   Page **6**

Section A—Allocation and Capitalization Methods (See page 4 of the instructions.)

Attach a description (including sample computations) of the present and proposed method(s) the applicant uses to capitalize direct and indirect costs properly allocable to property produced or acquired for resale. Include a description of the method(s) used for allocating indirect costs to intermediate cost objectives such as departments or activities prior to the allocation of such costs to property produced or acquired for resale. The description must include the following information.

1. The method of allocating direct and indirect costs (specific identification method; burden rate method; standard cost method; or other reasonable allocation method).
2. The method of allocating mixed service costs (direct reallocation method; step-allocation method; simplified service cost method using the labor-based allocation ratio; or the simplified service cost method using the production cost allocation ratio).
3. The method of capitalizing additional section 263A costs (simplified production method with or without the historic absorption ratio election; simplified resale method with or without the historic absorption ratio election including permissible variations; or the U.S. ratio method).

Section B—Direct and Indirect Costs Required To Be Allocated (See Regulations under sections 263A and 451.)

		Present method	Proposed method
1	Direct material		
2	Direct labor		
3	Indirect labor		
4	Officers' compensation (not including selling activities)		
5	Pension and other related costs		
6	Employee benefits		
7	Indirect materials and supplies		
8	Purchasing costs		
9	Handling, processing, assembly, and repackaging costs		
10	Offsite storage and warehousing costs		
11	Depreciation, amortization, and cost recovery allowance for equipment and facilities placed in service and not temporarily idle		
12	Depletion		
13	Rent		
14	Taxes other than state, local, and foreign income taxes		
15	Insurance		
16	Utilities		
17	Maintenance and repairs that relate to a production, resale, or long-term contract activity		
18	Engineering and design costs (not including section 174 research and experimental expenses)		
19	Rework labor, scrap, and spoilage		
20	Tools and equipment		
21	Quality control and inspection		
22	Bidding expenses incurred in the solicitation of contracts awarded to the applicant		
23	Licensing and franchise costs		
24	Capitalizable service costs (including mixed service costs)		
25	Administrative costs (not including any costs of selling or any return on capital)		
26	Research and experimental expenses attributable to long-term contracts		
27	Interest		
28	Other costs (Attach a list of these costs)		

Section C—Other Costs Not Required To Be Allocated

1	Marketing, selling, advertising, and distribution expenses		
2	Research and experimental expenses not included on line 26 above		
3	Bidding expenses not included on line 22 above		
4	General and administrative costs not included in Section B above		
5	Income taxes		
6	Cost of strikes		
7	Warranty and product liability costs		
8	Section 179 costs		
9	On-site storage		
10	Depreciation, amortization, and cost recovery allowance not included on line 11 above		
11	Other costs (Attach a list of these costs)		

Form 3115 - Application for Change in Accounting Method (page 6)

Form 3115 (Rev. 2-96)

Schedule D—Change in Reporting Advance Payments and Depreciation/Amortization

Part I   Change in Reporting Advance Payments (See page 4 of the instructions.)

1. If the applicant is requesting to defer advance payment for services under Rev. Proc. 71-21, 1971-2 C.B. 549, attach the following information.
   a. Sample copies of all service agreements used by the applicant that are subject to the requested change in accounting method. Indicate the particular parts of the service agreement that require the taxpayer to perform services.
   b. If any parts or materials are provided, explain how the parts or materials relate to the services provided and provide the cost of such parts or materials as an absolute number and a percentage of the contract price.
   c. If the change relates to contingent service contracts, explain how the contracts relate to merchandise that is sold, leased, installed, or constructed by the applicant and whether the applicant offers to sell, lease, install, or construct without the service agreement.
   d. A description of the method the applicant will use to determine the amount of income earned each year on contingent contracts and why that method clearly reflects income earned and related expenses in each year.

2. If the applicant is requesting a deferral of advance payments for goods under Regulations section 1.451-5, attach the following information.
   a. Sample copies of all agreements for goods or items requiring advance payments used by the applicant that are subject to the requested change in accounting method. Indicate the particular parts of the agreement that require the applicant to provide goods or items.
   b. A statement providing that the entire advance payment is for goods or items. If not entirely for goods or items, a statement that an amount equal to 95% of the total contract price is properly allocable to the obligation to provide activities described in Regulations section 1.451-5(a)(1)(i) or (ii) (including services as an integral part of those activities).

Part II   Change in Depreciation or Amortization (See page 4 of the instructions.)

Applicants requesting approval to change their method of accounting for depreciation or amortization complete this section. Supply this information for each item or class of property for which a change is requested.

*Note: If the property has been disposed of before the beginning of the year of change, a method change is not permitted for that property. See **Automatic change for section 167 property** in the instructions for Part II, Schedule D, on page 4, for information regarding automatic changes under Rev. Proc. 74-11, 1974-1 C.B. 420. Also in Part II, see **When Not To File Form 3115** for information concerning retroactive elections and election revocations.*

1. Is depreciation for the property figured under Regulations section 1.167(a)-11 (CLADR)? .... ☐ Yes ☐ No
   If "Yes," the only changes permitted are under Regulations section 1.167(a)-11(c)(1)(iii).
2. Is any of the depreciation or amortization required to be capitalized under any Code section (e.g., section 263A)? ☐ Yes ☐ No
   If "Yes," enter the applicable section ▶ ....
3. Has a depreciation or amortization election been made for the property (e.g., the election under section 168(f)(1))? ☐ Yes ☐ No
   If "Yes," state the election made ▶ ....
4. a. To the extent not already provided, describe the property being changed. Include in the description the type of property, the year the property was placed in service, and the property's use in the applicant's trade or business or income-producing activity.
   b. If the property is residential rental property, did the applicant live in the property before renting it? .... ☐ Yes ☐ No
   c. Is the property public utility property? . . . . ☐ Yes ☐ No
5. To the extent not already provided in the applicant's description of its present method, explain how the property is treated under the applicant's present method (e.g., depreciable property, inventory property, supplies under Regulations section 1.162-3, nondepreciable section 263(a) property, property deductible as a current expense, etc.).
6. If the property is not currently treated as depreciable or amortizable property, provide the facts supporting the proposed change to depreciate or amortize the property.
7. If the property is currently treated and/or will be treated as depreciable or amortizable property, provide the following information under both the present (if applicable) and proposed methods.
   a. The Code section under which the property is depreciated or amortized (e.g., section 168(g)).
   b. If the property is depreciated under section 168, identify the applicable asset class in Rev. Proc. 87-56, 1987-2 C.B. 674. (If none, state so and explain why.) Also provide the facts supporting the asset class under the proposed method.
   c. The depreciation or amortization method of the property, including the applicable Code section (e.g., 200% declining balance method under section 168(b)(1)).
   d. The useful life, recovery period, or amortization period of the property.
   e. The applicable convention of the property.

APPENDIX E
Jargon

A

Accountant: A person who inspects, keeps or adjusts accounts.

Accounting: The principle or practice of systematically recording, presenting and interpreting financial accounts.

Accounts Payable: The amount owed by your business to creditors or vendors; usually for goods or services.

Accounts Receivable: The amount owed to your business by clients or customers; usually for goods or services.

Accrual Accounting Method: The accounting method of reporting income in the year earned and deducting or capitalizing the expenses in the year incurred.

Annual Accounting Year: Twelve consecutive months beginning January 1 and ending December 31.

Assets: Things or resources owned by your business. A property or investment having monetary value that can be realized if sold.

Audit Trail: A sequence of references to a specific record or account that makes it feasible to track information about your business transactions.

B

Balance Sheet: A financial statement summarizing the assets, liabilities, and net worth of an individual or a business at a given date.

Bank Statement: A report provided by your financial institution showing the activity of your accounts for a given time period (usually monthly).

Bookkeeper: A person who keeps a systematic record of business transactions.

Bookkeeping: The work involved in keeping a systematic record of business transactions.

C

Calendar Year: *see* Annual Accounting Year.

Cash Accounting Method: The accounting method of reporting your revenues and expenses at the time they are actually received or paid.

Cash on Hand: Money that you have on hand, including petty cash. This does not include money in bank accounts.

Creditor: A company or individual who extends credit or to whom your business owes money.

Current Assets: Items that can be converted into cash within one year of the date on your net worth sheet. Usually referred to as *liquidable cash*.

Current Liabilities: Obligations payable within one operation cycle (usually a fiscal year).

D

Depreciation: Spreading the cost of business property (with a useful life of more than a year) over more than one tax year and deducting part of it each year.

Double entry accounting: Accounting system where each transaction is recorded twice. The premise is that each transaction is recorded such that it balances out to zero.

E

Equity: The net worth of a business. It represents the amount after you subtract your liabilities from your assets.

Expenses: The costs of doing business, which constitutes an outflow of assets. Expenses may flow out in the form of cash or credit cards, or by incurring accounts payable.

F

Fiscal Year: Twelve consecutive months ending on the last day of any month except December.

Fixed Assets: Resources owned by a business but not used for resale. These items are depreciable over a period of time which is determined by its expected useful life.

Fixed Assets Record: Record used to list and track depreciation requirements for the fixed assets of your business.

G

General Journal: Used with the double entry accounting system to record all business transactions in chronological order.

General Ledger: Entries made from the general journal that are posted into their appropriate expense category.

I

Income: The monies of other gain received in a given period by an individual or business for labor of services.

Income Statement: Also known as profit and loss statement. A financial statement that summarizes the various transactions of a business during a specified period, showing net profit or loss.

Interest Payable: Interest accrued on loans and credit.

Inventory: Raw materials, works in process, and goods manufactured or purchased for resale.

Invoice: A written record representing a sale (of goods or services).

IRS: Internal Revenue Service.

L

Liabilities: The debts of a person or business, as notes payable or long-term debts.

Long-Term Liabilities: Outstanding balances minus the current portion due (business loans, mortgages, leases, etc.).

N

Net Worth: The value of a business determined by the difference in liabilities and assets of the business. *See also* Owner's Equity.

Note: Written promise with terms for payment of a debt.

Notes payable: Short-term notes. Those that are due in a time period of less than one year.

O

Owner's Equity: The total investment into a business plus or minus profits or losses of the business. Often equated with net worth.

P

Petty Cash: Money deposited to the petty cash account and not yet spent; purchases made with cash or personal check because of the inconvenience of paying with a business check.

Prepaid Expenses: Goods or services rented or purchased prior to use. Examples of prepaid expenses include rent, insurance, etc.

Profit and Loss Statement: *see* Income Statement.

S

Schedule C: Part of IRS Form 1040 used to report profit and loss from a sole proprietorship business.

Self-Employment Tax: Social Security and Medicare tax for individuals who work for themselves.

Service-Oriented Business: A business that provides primarily services rather than products to its clients.

Short-Term Investments: Items planned to be converted to cash within a year (e.g., CDs, stocks, bonds, etc.).

Single entry accounting: Accounting system that deals with income and expenses.

Sole Proprietorship: A business owned and operated by a single individual (often a married couple). The most common form of legal structure for new small businesses.

T

Tax year: The annual accounting period you use for keeping your records and reporting your income and expenses.

Taxes Payable: Estimated tax amounts incurred during your established accounting period.

V

Vendor: One who vends or sells and to whom your business may owe money.

INDEX

A

accountant, 1, 3, 9, 14, 71
accounting methods, 22 42, 64, 66
    accural, 20
    cash, 20
    changes in, 22
    combination or hybrid, 20
    definition of, 20
    special, 20
    types of, 20
accounting periods
    calendar year, 19
    fiscal year, 19
accounting service, 71
accounting software, 5, 7, 40, 69
accounting systems, 66
    double entry, 14
    single entry, 14
accounts payable, 23, 41, 42
    sample record, 33
accounts receivable, 23, 33, 41, 42
    sample record, 32
accrual accounting method, 19, 66
    definition of, 20
    examples of, 21
assets, 40, 58, 66
    current, 41
    fixed, 41

B

balance sheet, 23, 40, 42, 58, 66
    sample, 41
bookkeeper, 1, 7, 9, 14, 71
bookkeeping service, 71
business
    checking account, 7, 68
    credit card, 68
    savings account, 68

C

calendar tax year
    definition of, 19
    requirements of , 19
cash accounting method, 21, 32, 66
    definition of, 20
    examples of, 20
cash on hand, 28, 41
client records, 45, 66
    benefits of keeping, 46
combination accounting method,
    definition of, 21
CPA, 7
creditors, 33
current assets, 41
current liabilities, 41

D

databases
    client, 46
    vendor, 47
depreciation
    definition of, 30
double entry accounting, 14, 16, 66
    definition of, 15

E

entertainment, 23, 38-39
estimated tax, 64-65,
expense, 20, 23, 59
    invalid, 26
    necessary, 26
    ordinary, 26
    valid, 26
expense record, 26, 42, 57
    sample, 27
expense summary, 29
    sample, 57

F

financial statement, 58
fiscal tax year
    definition of, 19
    requirements of, 19
fixed assets, 23, 41-42
    examples of, 30
    sample record, 31
form 1040, 1
    1040-ES, 64
    1128, 19
    3115, 22
    4562, 64
    8829, 64

G

general journal
    definition of, 15
general ledger
    definition of, 15

H

home-based business, 3, 14
hybrid accounting method, 21

I

income, 20, 23, 42, 56, 59, 66
    invalid, 24
    sample record, 25
    valid, 24
income summary, 56
interest payable, 41
inventory, 19
investments
    short-term, 41
    long-term, 41
IRS publications
    #225, 21
    #334, 21, 24, 26, 35, 39, 63, 69
    #463, 36
    #509, 64
    #534, 30
    #535, 21
    #537, 21
    #538, 21
    #917, 35
    #946, 21, 30
IRS tax forms, 103-132

J

Jargon, 133-137

L

liabilities, 40, 58
    current, 41
    long-term, 41
long-term investments, 41
long-term liabilities, 41

M

meals, 23, 38, 42, 66
    sample record, 39
mileage, 34, 72

N

net worth, 23, 40, 42
    calculation of, 40-41

P

petty cash, 28, 41, 42, 66
    sample record, 29
profit and loss statement, 58
    sample, 59

R

recordkeeping, 1-2, 4-5, 7, 9, 14, 35, 40, 42, 55, 65
    purpose of, 19
records, 19, 66, 70
    adequate, 68
    creating & maintaining, 22
    definition of, 23
    client, 45
    reasons to keep, 13

vendor, 45
references and resources
    accounting software, 95
    books, 91-92
    other sources, 98
    periodicals & publications, 93-94
    websites, 96-97

S

Schedule C, 1, 27, 63, 69
Schedule SE, 63
self-employment taxes, 63
service-oriented business, 1, 2, 14, 20, 24, 46, 51
    advantages of, 3
    definition of, 3
service list, 51, 66
    sample, 52
services
    corporate, 4
    examples, 3-4
    personal, 4
short-term investments, 41
single entry accounting, 16, 66
    definition of, 14
small business, 3, 14-15
social security
    tax id number, 7
software
    accounting, 5, 7, 40, 69
sole proprietor, 1, 3, 15, 19-20, 24, 64-65
    advantages of, 2
    definition of, 2
    disadvantages of, 2
special accounting method, 21
standard mileage rate, 34, 72
suggested IRS publications, 99-102

T

tax
    categories, 68
    estimated,
    identification number, 7
    federal, 41
    payable, 41
    schedule, 65
    self-employment, 41
    state, 41
tax calendar, 42, 66
    calendar year, 19
    changing, 19
    definition of, 19
    fiscal year, 19
transportation, 23, 42, 66
    actual expense, 34
    sample record, 35
    standard mileage rate, 34
travel, 23, 36, 42, 66
    sample record, 37

V

vendor, 33, 47, 66
    sample record, 47

W

worksheets, 73 - 89

ADDITIONAL INFORMATION

Comments & Suggestions
We welcome any feedback about this workbook as well as information to be considered for inclusion into any *Organize Your Books in 6 Easy Steps* sequels.

Bulk Ordering
Special rates are available for bulk ordering of books from IRIE Publishing for resale by conferences and seminars, professional organizations, or government agencies.

Other Publications
IRIE Publishing has several other publications available to assist the small and home-based business owner. Please refer to the order form for the titles of these publications. You may also contact us to receive a *free* copy of our catalog.

Seminars
In addition to her work as an organizational consultant and a researcher, Donna M. Murphy conducts seminars. Her topics include Clutter Management, Starting a Home-Based Business and Organizing Your Books. Please contact us if you would like more information on any of these seminars. Donna is also available to present special seminars or workshops at conferences, tradeshows or other events. Please contact her through IRIE Publishing.

IRIE Publishing
301 Boardwalk Drive
P.O. Box 273123
Fort Collins, CO 80527-3123

ORDER FORM

To order additional copies of Organize Your Books in 6 Easy Steps, check with your local bookstore, call, e-mail, or use the order form below.

Please send:

_____ copies of *Organize Your Books in 6 Easy Steps* (ISBN 0-9664848-0-0) @ $16.95 ea. $_____

_____ copies of Step-by-Step Guide to *Creatively Managing Clutter* @ $5.95 ea. $_____

_____ copies of Step-by-Step Guide to *Starting a Home-Based Business* @ $5.95 ea. $_____

_____ copies of Donna Murphy's newsletter *small office COMPENDIUM* @ $9.00. $_____

        Subtotal $_____
        Sales tax *(CO residents please add 3%)* $_____
        Shipping

            Books - add $3.00 for first book; $1.00 for each add'l book
            Booklets - add $1.00 for quantities of 1-99
            Newsletter - shipping included $_____

                                      Total $_____

Payment method:
_____ Check
_____ Money Order

Please ship to:
    Name: _____
    Company: _____
    Address: _____
    City/State/Zip: _____
    Phone: _____

IRIE PUBLISHING

301 BOARDWALK DRIVE
PO BOX 273123
FORT COLLINS, CO 80527
E-mail: iriepub@verinet.com

Thank you for your order!   (970) 482-4402

Here's What People Are Saying About

Organize Your Books In 6 Easy Steps: A Workbook for the Sole Proprietor Service-Oriented Business

Cash flow mis-management and problems with the IRS for bad record-keeping are the primary reasons small business owners go out of business. "*Organize Your Books In 6 Easy Steps*" is an easy read and good primer for the CEO of a small business. A must read!

— Cheryl D. Broussard, Author
Sister CEO, & The Black Woman's Guide to Financial Independence

"*Organize Your Books In 6 Easy Steps*" is great! It is just what the novice entrepreneur needs. In our 13 years in business, we have been through many trials and errors. We overcame a lot of the administrative headaches during startup. Your book would have eased those pains.

— James C. Smith, President
SEMA Incorporated